THE EXPANDING NEWS DESERT

By Penelope Muse Abernathy,
Knight Chair in Journalism and Digital Media Economics

The Center for Innovation and Sustainability in Local Media

School of Media and Journalism

University of North Carolina at Chapel Hill

© 2018 Center for Innovation and Sustainability in Local Media,
University of North Carolina at Chapel Hill

ISBN 978-1-4696-5324-2 (pbk.: alk. paper)
ISBN 978-1-4696-5325-9 (ebook)

Distributed by the University of North Carolina Press
116 South Boundary Street
Chapel Hill, NC 27514-3808
uncpress.org

CONTENTS

PREFACE

From our very beginnings as a nation, newspapers have played a vital role in building community. Strong newspapers fostered a sense of geographic identity and in the process nurtured social cohesion and grassroots political activism. The stories and editorials they published helped set the agenda for debate of important issues, influence the policy and political decisions we made, and build trust in our institutions. The advertisements they carried drove local commerce and regional economic growth by putting potential customers together with local businesses. Ron Heifetz, professor at Harvard University's John F. Kennedy School of Government, describes a newspaper as "an anchor" because it "reminds a community every day of its collective identity, the stake we have in one another and the lessons of our history. "

For residents in thousands of communities across the country – inner-city neighborhoods, affluent suburbs and rural towns– local newspapers have been the prime, if not sole, source of credible and comprehensive news and information that can affect the quality of their everyday lives. Yet, in the past decade and a half, nearly one in five newspapers has disappeared, and countless others have become shells – or "ghosts" – of themselves.

Since publishing The Rise of a New Media Baron and The Emerging Threat of News Deserts in 2016, we have continued to quantify the loss of our country's newspapers and considerably expand the information in our proprietary database of more than 9,000 newspapers. Our 2018 report, The Expanding News Desert, delves deeper into the implications for communities at risk of losing their primary source of credible news. Concerned citizens, community activists, philanthropists, policy makers, educators, journalists and others in the industry can use our website – **usnewsdeserts.com** – to drill down to the county level to understand how the news landscape in each of our 50 states has changed in recent years and the implications this has for their communities. By documenting the shifting news landscape and evaluating the threat of media deserts, our reports seek to raise awareness of the role each of these interested parties can play in addressing the challenges confronting local news and democracy.

Our 2018 edition consists of two separate reports – "The Loss of Local News: What It Means for Communities" and "The Enduring Legacy of Our New Media Barons: How They Changed the News Landscape."

"The Loss of Local News" documents the continuing loss of papers and readers, the consolidation in the industry, and the social, political and economic consequences for thousands of communities throughout the country. Our research found a net loss since 2004 of almost 1,800 local newspapers. We have also begun to identify papers where the editorial mission and staffing have been so significantly diminished that their newsrooms are either nonexistent or lack the resources to adequately cover their communities. Finally, we assess some of the recent efforts being made by other media – ranging from television stations to digital entrepreneurs – trying to fill the void that is left when a local newspaper dies and consider what still needs to be done.

"The Enduring Legacy of Our New Media Barons" provides an update on the strategies of the seven large investment firms – hedge and pension funds, as well as private and publicly traded equity groups – that swooped in to purchase hundreds of newspapers in recent years. It also explores the indelible mark they have left on the newspaper industry during a time of immense disruption.

The stakes are high, not just for the communities that have lost newspapers — or are living with the threat of losing a local newspaper – but also for the entire country. Our sense of community and our trust in democracy at all levels suffer when journalism is lost or diminished. In an age of fake news and divisive politics, the fate of communities across the country – and of grassroots democracy itself – is linked to the vitality of local journalism.

THE LOSS OF LOCAL NEWS:
WHAT IT MEANS
FOR COMMUNITIES

The past 15 years have been pivotal for the newspaper industry, a period of immense disruption and financial distress that reversed the good fortunes of the previous two decades. In 2004, newsroom employment and print advertising were near peak 1990s levels. Since then, the number of journalists employed by newspapers has been cut in half, and print advertising revenue has fallen to record low levels. The large metro and regional state papers felt the squeeze first. But by 2010, even century-old weeklies that had survived the Great Depression were feeling the existential threat. The question that hangs in the air today: Can local newspapers remain economically viable in the 21st century, overcoming a secular shift to digital by readers and advertisers and the resulting damage to the business models that have sustained them for 200 years.

Newspapers have been variously described as watchdogs that hold our civic institutions accountable and "furnish that check upon government which no constitution has ever been able to provide." "The bible of democracy, the book out of which a people determines its conduct." "Vitamin supplements for their communities and more" that provide the vast majority of "news that feeds our democracy" and "link people overwhelmed by otherness and isolation."[1]

What is at stake if we lose the thousands of local newspapers that have historically provided coverage of our cities and countryside? Numerous government and foundation studies have found that for a community to reach its full potential, it must be civically healthy and inclusive. Economists call public service journalism a "public good" because the information conveyed through news stories helps guide decision-making in our society. A 2011 report by the Federal Communications Commission found that local newspapers are the best medium to provide the sort of public service journalism that shines a light on the major issues confronting communities and gives residents the information they need to solve their problems. But, in many communities today, there is simply not enough digital or print revenue to pay for the public service journalism that local newspapers have historically provided. Therefore, the fate of communities and the vitality of local news – whether delivered over the internet, the airwaves or in print – are intrinsically linked.[2]

This report explores the loss and diminishment of local newspapers, the implications for our communities and our democracy, and the potential to thwart the rise of news deserts. The report is divided into five sections:

The Loss of Newspapers and Readers:
More than one in five papers has closed over the past decade and a half, leaving thousands of our communities at risk of becoming news deserts. Half of the 3,143 counties[3] in the country now have only one newspaper, usually a small weekly, attempting to cover its various communities. Almost 200 counties in the country have no newspaper at all. The people with the least access to local news are often the most vulnerable – the poorest, least educated and most isolated.

The Rise of the Ghost Newspaper:
In an era of fake news, the diminishment of local newspapers poses yet another threat to the long-term vitality of communities. Many of our 7,100 surviving newspapers are mere shells, or "ghosts," of their former selves. Once stand-alone iconic weeklies have merged with larger dailies and gradually disappeared. Metro, regional and state papers have dramatically scaled back their coverage of city neighborhoods, the suburbs and rural areas, dealing a double blow to communities that have also lost a local weekly

Bigger and Bigger They Grow:
Ownership matters, since it determines not only the editorial vision and mission of a newspaper, but also the future business models that will evolve for an industry in the midst of massive disruption. More than half of all newspapers have changed ownership in the past decade, some multiple times. The largest 25 newspaper chains own a third of all newspapers, including two-thirds of the country's 1,200 dailies. Not surprisingly, the number of independent owners has declined significantly in recent years, as family-owned papers have thrown in the towel and sold to the big guys. The consolidation in the industry places decisions about the future of individual papers, as well as the communities where they are located, into the hands of owners with no direct stake in the outcome.

Filling the Local News Void:
A range of entrepreneurs – from journalists at television stations to founders of digital sites – are experimenting with new business models and new ways of providing local news to hundreds of communities that have lost their local newspapers. Most ventures, however, are clustered around major metro areas. As a result, between 1,300 and 1,400 communities that had newspapers of their own in 2004 now have no local news coverage at all.

The Challenges and Opportunities That Remain:
There are no easy fixes. Despite this, for-profit and nonprofit ventures, as well as legacy and digital news organizations, are beginning to develop viable economic and journalistic models. The opportunity – and the challenge – is finding a way to scale these efforts so the thousands of communities that have lost a newspaper have a viable alternative. We need to make sure that whatever replaces the 20th century version of local newspapers serves the same community-building functions. If we can figure out how to craft and implement sustainable news business models in our smallest, poorest markets, we can then empower journalistic entrepreneurs to revive and restore trust in media from the grassroots level up, in whatever form – print, broadcast or digital.

Our findings are based on analysis of the data collected by the School of Media and Journalism at the University of North Carolina at Chapel Hill over the past four years. Our 2016 report was based on analysis of two industry databases that track newspapers. For our 2018 report, we have added three more layers of verification to determine the status of the more than 9,000 publications in our database, including information obtained from 55 state, regional and national press associations and our own extensive independent online research and interviews with staff at individual papers. Additionally, we added layers of demographic, political and economic data from government sources. As a result, you can use our website – **usnewsdeserts.com** – to drill down to the county level in every state to find out how your community has been affected. As was the case with the 2016 report, because our focus is on local newspapers, we have excluded from our analysis the country's largest national papers – The New York Times, Wall Street Journal and USA Today – as well as shoppers, magazines and other specialty publications, such as business journals.

THE LOSS OF NEWSPAPERS AND READERS

In our connected age, there is an abundance of news and opinion, coming at us 24/7. The latest terror attack, the presidential debates or the shenanigans of celebrities. It's all covered in minute detail, and we are free to share it and our opinions on the matter. But missing from that motley collection of trivia and substance is news of what is happening in our own backyards, save the personal videos posted by friends. Local news about a tax increase or a zoning decision is rarely of such interest that it trends, but it has an outsized impact on the everyday lives of residents in small towns, city neighborhoods and suburbia. When local newspapers fail, these communities are often left without any news organization to care about, watch over and report on the actions of the county commission or the local school board.

To better determine the impact that the loss of a local newspaper has on a community, researchers at UNC's School of Media and Journalism have spent the past two years collecting additional information on the more than 9,000 local papers in our proprietary database. This analysis found an unrelenting loss of newspapers and readers since 2004 with troubling implications for thousands of communities. While there are entrepreneurs who are beginning to fill the void that is left in a community when a newspaper fails, much more needs to be done.

Here are the major findings:

Vanishing Newspapers
The United States has lost almost 1,800 papers since 2004, including more than 60 dailies and 1,700 weeklies. Roughly half of the remaining 7,112 in the country – 1,283 dailies and 5,829 weeklies – are located in small and rural communities. The vast majority – around 5,500 – have a circulation of less than 15,000.

Vanishing Readers
Print readers are disappearing at an even faster rate than print newspapers, and the pace appears to be accelerating. Over the past 15 years, total weekday circulation - which includes both dailies and weeklies – declined from 122 million to 73 million. While more and more readers prefer to receive news online, this dramatic loss has been driven not only by changes in reader preference, but also by the business decisions of newspaper owners. The decrease in daily circulation comes primarily from the pullback of metro and regional newspapers from distribution to outlying rural and suburban areas. In contrast, much of the loss in weekly circulation since 2004 comes from the closure of more than 1,700 weeklies. This decrease in print readers raises serious questions about the long-term financial sustainability of both small community and large metro newspapers.

Who Lost the Most?
No state has been spared the death of a newspaper. California lost the most dailies of any state. Some of the most populated states – New York, Illinois and Texas — lost the most weeklies. The loss of newspapers in one state has the potential to affect residents in many other states, since government agencies often rely on local news reports to help identify and contain public health crises and assess the impact of environmental disasters.

Living Without a Newspaper
There are hundreds -- if not thousands – of communities at risk of becoming isolated news deserts. There are almost 200 of the 3,143 counties in the United States without any paper. An additional 1,449 counties, ranging in size from several hundred residents to more than a million, have only one newspaper, usually a weekly. More than 2,000 have no daily paper. The residents of America's emerging news deserts are often its most vulnerable citizens. They are generally poorer, older and less educated than the average American.

Silence in the Suburbs
Seventy percent – 1,300 – of the newspapers that closed or merged were in metro areas. All but 50 were weeklies, most with a circulation under 10,000. Their demise leaves a news vacuum for many of America's suburbs and urban neighborhoods, where residents have historically relied on community weeklies to keep them informed about the most pressing hyperlocal issues.

The Death of the Rural Hometown Newspaper
More than 500 newspapers have been closed or merged in rural communities since 2004. Most of these counties where newspapers closed have poverty rates significantly above the national average. Because of the isolated nature of these communities, there is little to fill the void when the paper closes.

The Shrinking State and Regional Newspapers
The dramatic pullback in circulation and coverage of state and regional papers has dealt a double blow to residents of outlying rural counties, as well as close-in suburban areas. Many of these communities have also lost their weekly hometown paper and are left without any credible and comprehensive sources of either local or regional political and economic news.

And Then There Was One
Fewer than a dozen cities of any size have two competing dailies. The lack of competition among newspapers in major metro markets often results in less coverage of local and state government, and residents of those cities pay the price. Studies have found that closure of a competing metro daily often leads to governmental inefficiency and higher costs for city residents.

VANISHING NEWSPAPERS

Cities and towns ranging in size from Lime Springs, Iowa, with a population of only 500, to Tampa, Florida, a city of 400,000 residents, have lost a hometown newspaper, as about one in five of the country's local papers has vanished in recent years. In total, the United States has lost almost 1,800 papers since 2004, including more than 60 dailies and 1,700 weeklies. Roughly half of the remaining 7,112 papers in the country – 1,283 dailies and 5,829 weeklies – are located in small and rural communities. The vast majority – around 5,500 – have circulations under 15,000. [4]

While closures of large dailies like The Tampa Tribune and the Rocky Mountain News in Denver grab headlines, in fact, 53 of the 62 dailies that closed or merged since 2004 had circulations of less than 50,000. Twenty of those shuttered dailies had a circulation of less than 5,000. This includes The Daily Times of Pryor Creek in rural northeastern Oklahoma.

Founded in 1919, The Times brought its 3,000 subscribers news "From Your Corner of the World to the World in Your Backyard." As circulation and advertising declined, the daily paper transitioned in 2013 to publishing only three times a week, in an effort to stave off closure. A small article above the fold of the Times' weekend edition on April 29, 2017, announcing that this was the last issue, shocked the 10,000 residents of Pryor Creek, the county seat. Almost a fourth of the 40,000 residents of Mayes County, named for a chief of the Cherokee Nation, live in poverty, and a fifth are Native Americans. [5] The shuttering of The Times leaves residents of Mayes County without a local newspaper. "You're going to see more and more papers go away because the advertising dollars are going away," said Jimmy Tramel, mayor of Pryor Creek. [6] "We have a huge communication gap in this country today, and I don't know what the answer is. It's a drastic blow to our city because, how do we get information out?"

Getting the information out is even more difficult for the 1,749 communities that have lost weeklies over the past 15 years. Weeklies are often the only

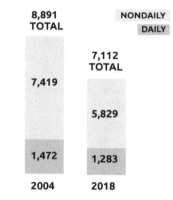

TOTAL NUMBER OF U.S. NEWSPAPERS: 2004 & 2018

There has been a net loss of 1,779 papers since 2004.
This net loss takes into account more than 100 dailies that shifted to weekly publication, as well as several dozen new weeklies that were established during that period. In total, 62 dailies and 1,749 weeklies closed or merged with other papers.

SOURCE: UNC Database

sources of very local news and information in communities – large and small, rich and poor, urban and rural. These shuttered weeklies ranged in size from the San Francisco Independent, with free distribution of almost 400,000, to the Sudan Beacon News in Texas, with a circulation of only 300. Of these closed or merged weeklies, only 45 had a circulation above 50,000. More than 1,000 had a circulation of less than 5,000.

Often these papers are shut with little notice. The staff and community of the 140-year-old, 500-circulation Gridley Herald, serving Gridley (population 6,000) in the central California county of Butte, were notified by their owners, GateHouse, on Aug. 29, 2018, that the final issue of the twice-weekly paper would be published the next day. Gridley, 60 miles from Sacramento, is largely an agricultural community. Half of the residents are Hispanic, in contrast to Butte County, which is predominantly white. [7]

Gridley is only sparsely covered by the neighboring daily, the Chico Enterprise-Record, located in a city with 90,000 residents, 30 miles away. "You lose a community when you don't have a newspaper," said one resident. Final stories in the Herald focused on a recent homicide; the opening of area schools, including the beginning of high school football season; and features on the Butte County Fair. "I'm especially saddened for the work we will not be able to do for you, the events we won't be covering . . .," noted the publisher, who had worked for the paper for 26 years, in the final edition.[8]

While there are more than 7,100 newspapers in still publishing as either weeklies or dailies, this count most likely overstates the number of stand-alone papers in existence today. Based on our analysis of the papers owned by the largest chains in the country, we estimate that between 10 and 20 percent of the papers in our database are geographically zoned weekly editions published by larger metro dailies. For example, the UNC database lists 158 papers owned by Digital First Media, the third-largest chain in the country. However, the website for Digital First lists fewer than 100 papers. Zoned editions are difficult to identify because they are listed separately as stand-alone weekly papers in various industry databases such as those compiled by Editor and Publisher and BIA Kelsey.

For our 2018 report, we have supplemented the information in industry databases with data obtained from all 50 state press associations and our own extensive independent online research and interviews with staff at individual papers. As a result, we identified 300 papers that were published in 2004, but were not included in national industry databases. Therefore, our 2004 number has been adjusted upward from our 2016 report to almost 8,900 papers. Simultaneously, we removed from our 2018 number the 600 papers that we identified as evolving from stand-alone newspapers into shoppers or lifestyle and business specialty publications, with little or no public service journalism. However, we left the zoned editions in the total of number of 7,112 papers since, even though they are not stand-alone newspapers, they are still – for the time being – providing a diet of local news that informs their respective communities. Recent history suggests that as the economics of print publishing continue to decline, many zoned editions will either become shoppers and specialty publications, or be eliminated entirely.

VANISHING READERS

Print readers are disappearing at an even faster rate than print newspapers, and the pace appears to be accelerating. Over the past 15 years, total weekday circulation — which includes both dailies and weeklies – declined 40 percent, from 122 million to 73 million, for a loss of 49 million. In the last four years alone, newspapers shed 20 million in circulation, an indication that the pace of the downward slide may be increasing.

This decrease in print readers speaks to the declining influence of newspapers, which once set the agenda for debate of important issues in their communities and helped encourage local economic growth and development. It also raises serious questions about the long-term financial sustainability of community newspapers, most of which still rely on print advertising and subscriptions for between 60 and 80 percent of their total revenue, and don't have the financial reserves that the large national and regional papers do.[9] As circulation declines and news coverage of outlying regions is cut back, print newspapers lose reach and relevance for both local advertisers and readers. This, in turn, drives down profitability and forces publishers to cut costs, instead of investing in ventures that will transform their print business models for the digital age.

The decline in daily circulation was driven by the largest dailies shedding existing readers, especially those in outlying areas. In 2018, only 53 dailies have a print circulation greater than 100,000, compared with nearly twice that many – 102 dailies – in 2004. Two-thirds of the 1,283 dailies still publishing have circulations under 15,000. If print circulation continues to drop at current rates, Nicco Mele, director of the Shorenstein Center for Media, Politics and Public Policy at Harvard University, predicts that as many as one-half of the nation's surviving dailies will no longer be in print by 2021.[10]

In contrast, the decline in weekly readership resulted primarily from the shuttering of 1,700 papers. The average circulation of the country's surviving 5,829 weeklies is 8,000, roughly the same as it was in 2004. However, print readership for both dailies and weeklies is probably much less than what is reported in industry databases. The Alliance for Audited Media (AAM) is the most authoritative source for circulation, but only 13 percent of papers in the UNC database – typically the largest papers – subscribe to AAM audits. More and more smaller newspapers — dailies as well as weeklies — are turning to self-reporting or not reporting their circulation numbers to sources such as Editor and Publisher. Additionally, the reported AAM numbers for the large dailies often lag behind the audit by a couple of years.

The dramatic circulation drop over the past 15 years occurred despite new rules and guidelines adopted by the industry after 2004 that allowed newspapers to count print and online readership that had previously been excluded.[11] Circulation statistics in the UNC database represent primarily print distribution, an admittedly imperfect measure since it does not count the increasing number of people who access local news online. However, readership data for most digital editions of the newspapers in this report are not widely available or comparable. Also, according to the Federal Communications Commission[12], between 40 and 60 percent of residents in rural areas lack reliable access to either broadband or wireless, therefore limiting their media options when a local print newspaper folds. Therefore, print circulation becomes a proxy – albeit imperfect – for the dramatic decline in influence and relevance of local papers in recent years.

TOTAL U.S. CIRCULATION: 2004 & 2018

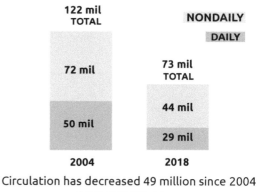

Circulation has decreased 49 million since 2004

SOURCE: UNC Database

WHO LOST THE MOST?

WHERE NEWSPAPERS HAVE CLOSED OR MERGED: 2004-2018

Frequency
- ■ Daily
- ■ Weekly

Since 2004, one-fifth of all U.S. newspapers have been closed or merged.
Source: UNC Database

No state has been spared the death of a newspaper. California lost the most dailies, 11, ranging in size from 22,000 to 157,000. This was primarily driven by consolidation in the San Francisco Bay Area. Over the course of five years, the third-largest newspaper chain in the country, Digital First, merged eight dailies into two mastheads: East Bay Times and Mercury News, which together currently reach nearly 300,000 subscribers. [13]

The more rural state of Kansas lost seven dailies, all with circulations under 10,000. The communities affected spanned the entire state, from the affluent Kansas City suburb of Overland Park to farmlands in Liberal, Kansas, in the southwest.

Some of the most populated states lost the most weeklies. Illinois lost 157, New York lost 155 and Texas lost 146. The weeklies in Illinois and New York were predominantly in the suburbs surrounding the large metro areas. This includes a chain of 35 independent weeklies in Suffolk County on Long Island, which were shuttered in 2008. In contrast, in Texas, nearly half of the weeklies closed were in rural counties.

The loss hit some states disproportionally, depending on how many papers they had. In 2004, the number of papers ranged from 14 in Hawaii to 638 in Texas. While Texas lost 146 papers, it still has almost 500 in 2018. The island state of Hawaii on the other hand, lost five of its 14 papers, including three weeklies and one daily on its most populated island of Oahu. In 2010, the two major dailies in Honolulu, the Honolulu Star-Bulletin and Honolulu Advertiser, merged to become the Star Advertiser,[14] robbing America of one of its last two-daily-newspaper towns.

The loss of newspapers in one state has the potential to affect residents in many other states, since government agencies often rely on local news reports to help identify and contain public health crises and assess the impact of natural and man-made disasters. Officials at the Centers for Disease Control and Prevention (CDC), for example, say that the death of newspapers throughout the country is already hindering their ability to spot and track the spread of disease, which could lead to outbreaks of more epidemics. [15] The CDC relies on the news stories in local papers to provide them with an early warning system, which is critical in containing the spread. So far, social media has been much less reliable.

LIVING WITHOUT A NEWSPAPER

NEWS DESERTS: COUNTIES WITHOUT NEWSPAPERS

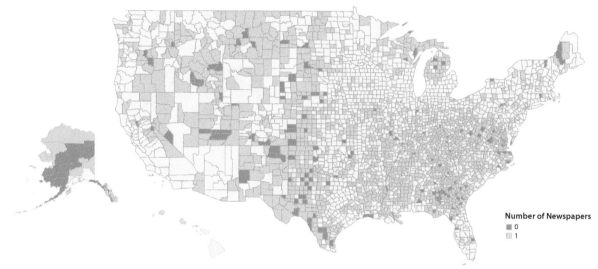

Number of Newspapers
- 0
- 1

In the U.S., 171 counties do not have a local newspaper.
Nearly half of all counties - 1,449 - have only one newspaper, usually a weekly.

As newspapers vanish and readers drop off, an increasing number of Americans are living without a reliable and comprehensive source of local news. Previously, we defined a "news desert" as a community without a local newspaper. As a result of the dramatic shrinkage in the number of local news outlets in recent years, as well as the decrease in local news coverage by surviving newspapers, we have expanded our designation of news deserts to include communities where residents are facing significantly diminished access to the sort of important news and information that feeds grassroots democracy.

There are hundreds — if not thousands – of communities at risk of becoming isolated news deserts. The numbers have grown dramatically in recent years as local newspapers vanish and nothing replaces them.

- There are almost 200 of the 3,143 counties in the United States without any paper – weekly or daily – creating a news vacuum for about 3.2 million residents and public officials in those counties.

- An additional 1,449 counties, ranging in size from several hundred residents to more than a million, have only one newspaper, usually a weekly that may struggle to find the resources to cover dozens of other communities in that county, spread out over many miles.

- And more than 2,000 counties do not have a daily newspaper, which means residents in those counties are mostly reliant on either social media or news outlets in adjacent counties or faraway cities for their daily news feed. These distant news outlets – daily metro newspapers, as well as regional television stations — provide only sporadic coverage of these counties without a daily paper, and social media outlets are, invariably, an unreliable source.[16]

The residents of America's emerging news deserts are often its most vulnerable citizens. They are generally poorer, older and less educated than the average American. They are much more likely to live in rural areas of the country. Eighteen percent

DEMOGRAPHIC PROFILES OF COUNTIES WITHOUT NEWSPAPERS

Demographic Measure	News Deserts	U.S.
Average Poverty Rate	18%	13%
Average Median Income ($/Year)	$45,000	$59,000
Average Median Age (Years)	42	38
Average Percent of Residents With Bachelor's Degree or Higher	19%	33%

Source: UNC Database and US Censu Bureau

of residents are living in poverty compared with the national average of 13 percent.[17] Fewer than 20 percent of residents of these counties have any college education, roughly half the nationwide average. Almost half of Americans living in a county without a newspaper also live in a food desert, which the U.S. Department of Agriculture defines as "parts of the country vapid of fresh fruit, vegetables, and other healthful whole foods, usually found in impoverished areas."[18]

Residents of low-income areas tend to be overlooked by advertisers are less likely to purchase subscriptions and have less access to both legacy and digital media, according to Stanford University economist James Hamilton. This has long-term social and economic consequences for rural communities. Since residents in news deserts tend to be less informed about key issues in their community, they are less likely to vote.[19]

The South had the most counties without newspapers: 91.[20] Almost every state in the South had at least one news desert. In Georgia 28 out of 169 counties did not have a newspaper and in Texas 22 out of 254 counties lacked a paper. Kentucky, Virginia, North Carolina, Tennessee, Florida and Oklahoma all had half a dozen or so counties without newspapers. Counties that recently lost their last surviving newspaper ranged from Jerome County, Idaho, with 22,000 residents, which lost its weekly paper in 2008, to Mayes County in Oklahoma, with 40,000 residents, which lost its once proud daily in 2017. Both counties have poverty rates significantly above the national average. The 1,449 counties with only one newspaper still publishing range from Arthur County, Nebraska, with 500 residents, to Montgomery County, Maryland, with more than a million people.

COUNTIES WITHOUT NEWSPAPERS BY REGION: 2018

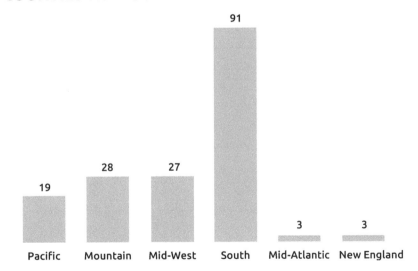

States were grouped into regions according to the following classifications: **Pacific:** AK, CA, HI, OR, WA; **Mountain:** AZ, CO, ID, MT, NV, NM, UT, WY; **Midwest:** IL, IN, MI, OH, WI, IA, KS, MN, MO, NE, ND, SD; **South:** DE, DC, FL, GA, MD, NC, SC, VA, WV, AL, KY, MS, TN, AR, LA, OK, TX; **Mid-Atlantic:** NJ, NY, PA; **New England:** CT, ME, MA, NH, RI, VT

SOURCE: UNC Database

SILENCE IN THE SUBURBS

Half of the newspapers that closed or merged were in large metro areas with more than 1 million people — such as Chicago, Washington, D.C., New York and Boston — and another 20 percent were in small and mid-sized metro areas such as Toledo, Ohio, and North Adams, Massachusetts. Of these 1,300 shuttered papers in metro areas, 1,250 were weeklies, most with a circulation under 10,000. Their demise leaves a news vacuum for America's suburbs and urban neighborhoods, where residents have historically relied on community weeklies to keep them informed about the most pressing issues – from test scores in local schools to proposed tax hikes. Both affluent and low-income suburban and metro areas were affected.

A number of factors drove the loss of the suburban papers. In many cases, as circulation declined and advertisers moved dollars from newspapers to broadcast and digital outlets, independent and family-run enterprises made the decision to cut their losses. In other cases, the corporate owner made either a strategic or financial decision to shutter the weeklies and invest elsewhere.

The tiny Baldwin City Signal in the college town of Baldwin City, Kansas, outside Kansas City, and the much larger Suffolk County Life, a chain of 35 papers on Long Island, New York, that reached several hundred thousand households, are examples of family-operated enterprises that did not survive.

The Signal was started in 1999 by the family-owned Lawrence Journal-World, located 15 miles away in Lawrence, home of the University of Kansas. In 2004, when it merged with another nearby paper, the Signal had a circulation of 1,700. By 2015, when it was shuttered[21] for lack of advertising and subscription revenue, it had fewer than 200 subscribers. Nevertheless, the closure has left

NUMBER OF NEWSPAPERS CLOSED OR MERGED IN METRO AND NON-METRO AREAS: 2004-2018

Metro Areas Categories	Number of Papers
Counties in metro areas with populations greater than 1 million	856
Counties in metro areas with populations from 250,000 to 1 million	276
Counties in metro areas with populations less than 250,000	162
Non-Metro Areas Categories	
Urban population of 20,000 or more, adjacent to a metro area	102
Urban population of 20,000 or more, not adjacent to a metro area	41
Urban population of 2,500 to 19,999, adjacent to a metro area	170
Urban population of 2,500 to 19,999, not adjacent to a metro area	114
Completely rural or less than 2,500 urban population, adjacent to a metro area	31
Completely rural or less than 2,500 urban population, not adjacent to a metro area	58
TOTAL	**1,810**

SOURCE: UNC Database and U.S. Department of Agriculture Economic Research Service

community leaders and activists scrambling to find new ways of "getting news out about important events and issues" to residents in Baldwin City, which is home to 4,600 residents and Baker University, the oldest college in Kansas. Despite its small circulation, the Signal served as a megaphone, since it was read by influential residents in Baldwin City who made sure they got out the vote on important issues. "We share one journalist with other communities. . . . There is no way he can be here [covering] the school board, city council and university and high school activities . . . and still cover other communities," one resident told a Kansas State University researcher. "Now I get news about things that will happen after they have already happened," said another.[22]

The Suffolk County Life papers were started in the 1960s, when Long Island was booming. The idea for the papers was hatched around the kitchen table of publisher and editor David Willmott's parents. His papers quickly gained journalistic accolades for coverage of the economic and environmental issues associated with a proposal to build a nuclear power plant on the shores of Long Island in the 1970s.[23] The power company ultimately abandoned plans to build the plant, citing public sentiment, which had turned against the plant in part because of the aggressive coverage that Willmott's papers provided. At their closing, the papers distributed more than 500,000 free copies and 10,700 paid copies.[24] In failing health and unable to find a buyer or a successor, Wilmott shuttered all the papers. His legacy – and that of his papers – was noted in a 2009 obituary that read "[Willmott] remained true to his views, ultimately becoming a weather vane for the electorate each November."[25]

In contrast to the local considerations that determined the demise of the Baldwin City and Suffolk papers, the closures of weeklies in the Chicago, Boston and Washington, D.C., suburbs were driven by the financial and strategic decisions made by corporate owners.

In 2009, the Chicago Sun-Times, faced with bankruptcy, shuttered more than a dozen of its weeklies[26], with a combined circulation of more than 200,000, most in predominantly affluent suburbs. These papers ranged in circulation from 1,000 to 27,000, including the 2,000 circulation Wheeling Countryside, which covered the 124-year-old village of 40,000 residents, 30 miles from downtown Chicago. Wheeling has one of the more diverse populations in the prestigious northern suburbs

of Chicago, with a third Hispanic and more than 15 percent Asian residents.[27] When announcing this closing, Larry Green, then publisher of the community weeklies, noted, "The death of any newspaper is a blow to our democracy and to your local economy. . .. But as much as it is a public service, the Wheeling Countryside is also a business. It must be profitable. In the current economy it is not."[28] Subscribers soon received a letter telling them how to subscribe to the Chicago Sun-Times, a daily covering an area of 3 million people with little specific content on a community like Wheeling.

Kirk Davis, CEO of GateHouse chain of papers, used a similar financial rationale in explaining the closure of 10 of its 125 weeklies in the Boston suburbs in 2013. All of the weeklies were in low-income neighborhoods that were not attractive to print advertisers. "Business conditions have become more challenging, and it's more important to be selective about where you're putting the greatest amount of resources," Davis told The Boston Globe. "We're going to shift resources to the highest potential markets that are most desirable to our advertisers."[29]

Corporate strategy also determined the fate of 20 Maryland papers, known as The Gazette, in the affluent Washington, D.C., suburbs of Montgomery and Prince George counties. The 55-year-old Gazette papers were purchased by The Washington Post in the early 1990s and distributed more than 450,000 free copies in 2014. Almost immediately after buying the Post in 2013, Jeff Bezos, the new owner, made the decision to shutter all the weeklies and instead devote his attention and financial resources to positioning the Washington Post as a national newspaper. "You lose that individual feel that our town matters," a Montgomery County resident said in a 2015 interview about the closing of The Gazette. "There are activities in our town that nobody can really convey to each other anymore when you lose that vehicle for getting the news out."[30]

DEATH OF THE RURAL HOMETOWN NEWSPAPER

More than 500 newspapers have been closed or merged in rural communities since 2004. The average circulation of the shuttered rural papers was roughly 4,000, highlighting the small size of communities they serve. In many of these communities, the local newspaper is the only reliable source of news and information. Because of the isolated nature of these communities, there is little to fill the void when the paper closes. A 2016 FCC Report found between 40 and 60 percent[31] of rural residents lacked affordable, high-speed access to wireless services that would enable streaming of videos, for example.

In rural counties where papers have closed or merged, the average poverty rate is nearly 4 percentage points higher than the national average of 12.7 percent. Sixty-two percent of voters in these rural counties voted for Trump in the 2016 election, compared with 46 percent nationwide.[32]

The economic challenges facing rural newspapers differ from those of their metro counterparts. These papers are often in small markets that are unattractive to advertisers outside of communities where the papers are located. Many of the papers that closed were independently owned and were forced to close when owners faced declining profits or couldn't find a buyer.

Lime Springs, Iowa, with a population of fewer than 500 residents, lost its 139-year-old weekly newspaper in 2015. In its last issue, dated Feb. 11, the Lime Springs Herald recalled the paper's expansive history, printing vintage ads dating back to 1897 and stories from readers about what the paper meant to them and to their community, located in Howard County in northeast Iowa, 200 miles from both Minneapolis and Des Moines. Carl Cassidy left an indelible mark on the paper, purchasing it when he was 19 and then serving as publisher, editor and community historian for 61 years.[33] In 1992, he sold it to the Evans family, who decided in 2015 to absorb it into their nearby 8,000-circulation weekly, the Cresco Times Plain Dealer. At the time of its closing, the Herald had a print circulation of 600. The last story published

CIRCULATION OF CLOSED OR MERGED RURAL PAPERS: 2004-2018

Circulation Range	Number of Rural Papers Closed or Merged
Greater than 15,000	28
5,001-15,000	91
5,000 or less	398

SOURCE: UNC Database

on its website was the Howard-Winneshiek School Board's 4-1 decision to close the Lime Springs elementary school.[34] "Small newspapers can't keep up," said Herald editor Marcie Klomp in a 2015 interview. "There is a place for a small newspaper, but I guess there isn't room for this one."[35]

In Missouri, the 104-year-old daily Macon Chronicle-Herald closed in 2014 when the neighboring family-owned newspaper, the Lewis County Press, purchased its assets from the GateHouse chain. For nearly 50 years, from 1926 to 1973, the paper was owned and edited by Frank P. Briggs, who served first as mayor of Macon and then as a state senator. When Harry Truman resigned his U.S. Senate seat in 1945, Briggs was appointed to serve out his term. In 1958, the University of Missouri, his alma mater, honored him and his long-running column, "It Seems to B," with a distinguished journalism award saying he had "achieved the nearly impossible feat of keeping his newspaper and his public responsibilities entirely divorced from one another."[36] Macon native Judy Baughman lamented the closure of the 1,700-circulation paper. "My wedding was in there; my engagement was in there," Baughman said. "At various times, my then-husband and my son were featured. . .. So it really breaks my heart that it's no longer in business."[37]

THE SHRINKING METRO AND STATE PAPERS

The dramatic pullback in circulation and coverage of state and regional papers has dealt a double blow to residents of outlying rural counties, as well as close-in suburban areas. Many of these communities have also lost their weekly hometown paper and are left without any credible and comprehensive sources of either local or regional political, economic and environmental news that can affect the quality of everyday life today and in the future.

In the latter half of the 20th century, when circulation and newsroom staffing were at their highest levels ever, major metro and state papers routinely received Pulitzer Prizes, the most coveted award in journalism, for their aggressive investigative reporting. The Philadelphia Inquirer, Los Angeles Times and Boston Globe, for example, had a cadre of reporters, stationed in Washington and abroad, who often scooped The New York Times and Washington Post on foreign and national news. But it was at the state and regional level where these large papers had their biggest impact on the quality of life for residents in the communities where they circulated. In North Carolina, for example, The News & Observer of Raleigh received the Pulitzer Public Service Award in 1996 for exposing the long-term environmental consequences of large-scale industrial hog farming on the state's rural counties[38], many of which were struggling economically.

By devoting a team of investigative reporters to the task of sifting through government records, analyzing data and then translating what they had found into lucid prose and compelling articles that consumed tons of newsprint, these large papers were able to set the agenda for debate of important policy issues that ultimately affected all residents in the state and region. On a day-to-day basis, the nation's large regional papers also had scores of reporters assigned to bureaus in the suburbs and outlying counties, who were responsible for staying on top of news at the grassroots level by covering the often mundane and routine government meetings that rarely made headlines outside the communities they were covering.

While editors at these papers believed they had a journalistic duty to cover regional issues, there was, no business model to support their expansive coverage. The vast majority of their financial support came from advertisers in their home city who had little desire or reason to reach consumers in these remote communities. Therefore, publishers began to take a hard look at the return on the investment from circulating print copies outside their metro area. Over the past two decades, this has led to dramatic cutbacks in both the circulation and staffing of the state and regional papers, the majority of them owned by the large newspaper chains, such as Gannett, McClatchy, Lee Enterprises and GateHouse. Since 2004, circulation for the large dailies has decreased by more than 40 percent and newsroom staffing by a similar amount.[39] A majority of the decline in daily circulation has resulted from the pullback of the large metros from rural areas.

Recent research has shown that when metro papers pull back circulation and coverage in outlying areas, participation and voting, especially in midterm state and local elections, goes down.[40] Additionally, there is evidence that the journalistic competition between metro papers and smaller community publications may spur more aggressive coverage of issues in these outlying communities since local reporters don't want to be scooped by the big-city journalists. This is especially true when metro papers assign reporters to cover routine governmental meetings in outlying areas.

The Wichita Eagle, the largest paper in Kansas, is representative of this decline in circulation, staffing and, ultimately, impact on the communities these papers covered. In the 1990s, The Eagle, then part of the Knight Ridder newspaper chain, gained national recognition for pioneering a new type of local reporting, called "civic journalism," which sought to engage readers in determining coverage of important issues in a community. Editors surveyed residents to get their input and then aggressively covered those issues – ranging from environmental concerns to tax increases – holding public officials accountable for resolving them. In the mid-1990s, the Eagle

DECLINE IN WICHITA EAGLE DISTRIBUTION: 1992-2018

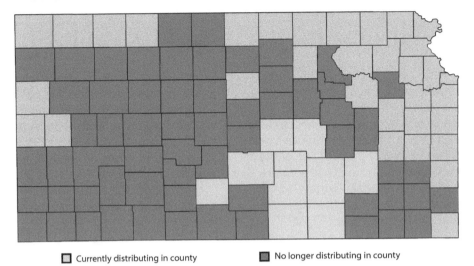

☐ Currently distributing in county   ■ No longer distributing in county

The Wichita Eagle circulates in just 10 counties in Kansas,
compared to more than 70 counties in 1992.

Source: Standard Rate and Data Service (SRDS)

had a circulation of 122,000and more than 100 journalists in its newsroom (including both a dedicated Washington reporter and a team of state and regional reporters). It was distributed in 73 of the state's 105 counties.[41] Today, the paper, which is now part of the McClatchy newspaper chain, has a print circulation of 30,000 and a newsroom of fewer than three dozen journalists. It circulates in only 10 counties).[42] The prominent three-story building in downtown Wichita that The Eagle once occupied has been sold to Cargill, and the newspaper has moved into a much smaller second-floor space in the restaurant and nightclub district. The Wichita paper is printed by The Kansas City Star, also a McClatchy paper, 200 miles away. Early printing deadlines make it difficult to offer timely coverage of both night sporting events and government meetings, and therefore lessens the relevance to readers and impact of the paper on the communities where it still circulates.

The story is the same across the country. The Portland Oregonian, which received the Pulitzer Public Service award in 2001 for its "detailed and unflinching examination" of immigration issues[43], has 158,000 circulation in 2018, but distributes to 15 fewer counties in Oregon and Washington than it did in 2004, when it had a circulation of 338,000. All but one of these counties no longer served by the Oregonian are rural, and all have poverty rates higher than the national average. The St. Louis Post-Dispatch, the flagship of the Pulitzer chain

until it was purchased by Lee Enterprises in 2005, has a current circulation of 150,000 and distributes to 30 fewer counties (17 fewer counties in Missouri and 13 fewer in the adjacent suburban counties of Illinois) than it did in 2004 when it had a circulation of almost 300,000. All of these counties have high poverty rates, and all but two are rural. The News & Observer, which had a circulation of 150,000 in the mid-1990s when it received the Pulitzer Prize for its nine-part series on commercial hog farming, has only 95,000 subscribers today and has pulled out of six counties in eastern North Carolina featured in the prize-winning articles.[44]

AND THEN THERE WAS ONE

The death of the two-newspaper town is yesterday's news. Nevertheless, as recently as a decade ago, there were still a dozen or so large cities with competing daily publications. However, the recession of 2008, coupled with the simultaneous shift in readership away from print newspapers to online news sources, has led to the demise of half of the remaining stalwarts. Only four of the 62 dailies lost since 2004 had circulations of more than 100,000. All four were in two-newspaper towns – Denver, Seattle, Honolulu and the Tampa/St Petersburg region.

In 2016, Florida's largest newspaper, the Tampa Bay Times in St. Petersburg (with a circulation of 200,000), purchased the competing daily Tampa Tribune in neighboring Hillsborough County (with 137,000 circulation), and quickly shut it down, leaving the Tampa Bay area of 3 million residents with only one newspaper. "The continued competition between the newspapers was threatening to both," Times chairman and CEO Paul Tash said in a statement. "There are very few cities that are able to sustain more than one daily newspaper, and the Tampa Bay region is not among them." [45]

The demise of the Tampa paper was preceded in 2009 and 2010 by the closure of three other large dailies. In 2010 the two remaining dailies in Honolulu merged to become the Honolulu Star-Advertiser (with a circulation of 153,000 in 2018). In 2009, the Rocky Mountain News in Denver, which had a circulation of 200,000, shut down[46], and the Seattle Post-Intelligencer (with circulation 120,000) transitioned to an online-only news site, leaving The Seattle Times (with circulation of 172,00 in 2018) as the primary news source for Washington's largest city.[47]

The lack of competition among newspapers in major metro markets often results in less coverage of local and state government. A report by the FCC on "The Information Needs of Communities" found that even in metro markets, with multiple media options including regional television stations and online outlets, the daily newspaper tended to provide most of the in-depth "watchdog" journalism.[48] This is because the metro paper typically had more reporters than the digital and broadcast news organizations and did not have the "on-air time constraints" imposed on morning and evening television newscasts, which typically devote more time to coverage of weather and sports than local policy issues.[49]

In a similar vein, research from the University of Notre Dame and University of Chicago found that the closure of a competing metro daily often leads to governmental inefficiency and higher costs for city residents. It specifically cited the journalism of the Rocky Mountain News, which had served as a vigilant watchdog for residents of Denver, providing them with information on how their tax dollars were spent. The stories covered by the News "included an audit of questionable federal funds allocated to the sheriff's department, a handshake deal between city government and Lufthansa Airlines, which may have violated federal law, lack of oversight for 390 'special taxing districts' established in the Denver metropolitan area, and an 'under-the-table' scheme at Denver International Airport that paid employees undeserved wages."[50]

Even if the metro paper transitions to online delivery – as the Seattle Post-Intelligencer did in 2009 – research suggests there is still a diminishment in both the quantity and quality of government news stories in the online versions.[51] As a result, residents in a community are likely to be less aware of the issues and less likely to vote in local elections.[52]

THE RISE OF
THE GHOST NEWSPAPER

As hundreds of small weeklies and dozens of dailies vanished from the U.S. news landscape in recent years, thousands of other dailies and weeklies became shells, or "ghosts," of their former selves. Many of these papers are still published – sometimes under the same name as in the past – but the quality, quantity and scope of their editorial content are significantly diminished. Routine government meetings are not covered, for example, leaving citizens with little information about proposed tax hikes, local candidates for office or important policy issues that must be decided.

Research by Duke University attempted to quantify the diminishment of local news by analyzing over 16,000 news stories provided to 100 randomly selected communities in one week. The study found that fewer than half of news stories provided to a typical community were produced by the local media outlet, and only 17 percent were about the community or events that took place there. The local news ecosystem seemed to be least robust in communities that had significant portions of Hispanic/Latino populations or in neighborhoods and suburbs that were either in, or adjacent to, large metro markets. The study also found that even when a local newspaper was located in a county seat, there was no increase in "journalistic production . . . [which] would seem to reinforce contemporary concerns about the decline in local government reporting." [53]

There are two paths to becoming a ghost newspaper:

In one scenario, **a weekly or small daily, often in a metro or suburban area, is purchased by a larger daily and slowly fades away as its news-gathering operations are merged with the larger paper's.** In its final stages of life, the once stand-alone weekly transitions to a free-distribution shopper or an upbeat lifestyle and entertainment publication. There is no breaking news or public service journalism. Between 2004 and 2018, almost 600 once-stand-alone newspapers – or one-third of the 1,800 papers that the country lost — became advertising supplements, free-distribution shoppers or lifestyle specialty publications.

In the second scenario, **newspapers become "ghosts" when their newsroom staffing is so dramatically pared back that the remaining journalists cannot adequately cover their communities.** In general, this has occurred among the nation's dailies and larger weeklies. Although the exact number is hard to pin down, we estimate, based on news accounts and industry data, at least 1,000 of the 7,200 newspapers still published in this country – and perhaps as many as 1,500 – have lost significantly more than half of their newsroom staffs since 2004. As a result, they have become ghosts, with drastically curtailed reach and journalistic missions.

Unlike the 600 weeklies that evolved into advertising supplements and were removed from the UNC database, the estimated 1,000 to 1,500 large dailies with drastically reduced editorial missions are counted in the overall total of 7,100 surviving newspapers. However, the sheer size of this contingent – and the fact that most are dailies – speaks to the magnitude of the diminishment of local news at the local, state and regional levels in recent years.

GOING, GOING GONE

A third of the 1,800 papers – 600 – that were lost over the past decade slowly faded away. Most were suburban weeklies. Like the frog in slowly boiling water, few people in the community noticed anything different at first. There was no abrupt closure that grabbed headlines. Often there was merely an announcement that the paper had been purchased by the owner of a nearby, larger daily.

Initially, the paper continued to be published under the same name, and the reporters who worked for the paper continued to aggressively cover local government. However, as circulation declined, the once stand-alone paper became a zoned edition of the larger paper. Over time, the building where the paper had been published for decades – often a landmark in the community – was sold and staffing dramatically reduced. Increasingly, news coverage focused on noncontroversial topics – lifestyle features on people and events in the community. In the final stage, management at the larger daily paper announced that the zoned edition would become a weekly specialty publication, advertising supplement in the main paper or a TMC (total market coverage) product or shopper, distributed free to all residents in the community.

UNC used a three-step process to identify these ghost newspapers. It included analysis of the editorial content of the newspapers, online research – especially focusing on official statements by corporate owners – as well as a comparison of our database of more than 9,000 newspapers with the current databases maintained by the country's 50 state press associations. The Casper Journal in Casper, Wyoming, (population 60,000) and the Smithfield Herald in Smithfield, North Carolina, (population 16,000) are representative of 600 metro and suburban weeklies that have transitioned from stand-alone, independent newspapers to ghost newspapers in recent years.

The Casper Journal was started in 1976 in Wyoming's second-largest city out of a perceived need to fill a gap in local news coverage left by

the Casper Star-Tribune, which was then owned by Howard Publications and circulated throughout the state. "We started our paper based on a niche we felt was left open by the Casper Star-Tribune," then Casper Journal publisher Dale Bohren said in an interview. Over the years, the weekly acquired a reputation for aggressive coverage of local issues, as well as elected officials. In 2003, the Journal was awarded second place for editorial excellence in the small-weeklies division by the state press association. The following year, it was purchased by the Casper Star-Tribune, now owned by Lee Enterprises. At first, all 13 members of the staff — including the publisher – remained on board to serve the publication's 30,000 readers. The publisher of the Star-Tribune stressed that the acquisition was not intended to end local competition, saying, "Whether you own one product or two in a marketplace, that does not diminish your responsibility to readers and advertisers."

But over the past 14 years, the news operations of the Journal have been completely merged with the Star-Tribune. In 2017, the Journal became a TMC advertising publication, distributed free to residents in the area. It features no unique or original local articles, according to the Wyoming Press Association. A note to readers promised that "this change means the Journal can now offer expanded news and sports coverage to keep you informed about what's happening in town and across Wyoming." However, a recent posting on the website of Casper Radio Station 95.5 expressed a different sentiment. It was titled, "Tired of the Casper Journal Littering Your Lawn? Here's How to Stop Delivery."[54]

The Smithfield Herald began publishing in 1882, the same year that the railroad arrived in Johnston County in eastern North Carolina. Throughout the 1900s, the family-owned paper located in the community of Smithfield, 30 miles from the state capital of Raleigh, received numerous journalism awards for its column writing and editorials, as well as its reporting on local news and high school sports. In 1980, the Raleigh News & Observer, which was then independently owned and operated by the Daniels family, purchased the Herald. Over the next three decades, The News & Observer, which was sold to McClatchy in 1995, acquired nine other community weeklies, including the Cary News, the Clayton News-Star and the storied 100-year-old Chapel Hill Newspaper, whose editor was immortalized in the nationally syndicated cartoon "Shoe." Over time, the news staffs at each of the weeklies were reduced until there was only one reporter covering each of the 10 communities, and the buildings where the papers were once published were sold. In 2017, citing financial reasons, McClatchy converted all 10 of these newspapers into advertising publications, titled "Triangle Today," distributed free to nonsubscribers and composed of "repurposed" entertainment, lifestyle and sports news, as well as syndicated columns. All 10 of these suburban Raleigh communities now rely on The News & Observer for primary coverage of local news. This means that routine city and county governmental meetings in these communities are no longer covered by any news outlet. [55]

The path of the almost 600 papers that followed this trajectory in becoming a ghost newspaper raises concerns about the future of the country's remaining 3,200 metro and suburban weeklies that are owned by larger metro and regional dailies. This includes, for example, the 23 Houston weeklies and one daily purchased by Hearst in 2016 from 10/13 Investments and merged into the Houston Chronicle as zoned editions. [56] As the economics of the metro and regional dailies continue to deteriorate, will many more suburban weeklies transition from zoned editions with local news to advertising publications without any local news?

THE COLLAPSE OF THE LARGE DAILIES

While weeklies in the country's suburbs and cities often fade into oblivion without anyone outside the community noticing, the layoffs at the large dailies often attract headlines in news outlets across the country. Many of the reporters laid off have been longtime business and investigative reporters who know how to write articles that attract attention and headlines.

This past year, after multiple rounds of cutbacks have left newsrooms that once employed hundreds with only a few dozen reporters and editors, reporters have been especially successful in calling attention to the diminished state of journalism at once-iconic dailies.

Recent internet postings by journalists have pointed out that over the past decade and a half, the U.S. lost more newspaper jobs than coal mining jobs – both in terms of numbers and percentages.[57] According to the Bureau of Labor Statistics, since 2004 employment in coal mining has declined 26 percent (from 70,558 to 51,866), while newspaper staffing has dropped 45 percent (from 71,640 to 39,210).[58] Other surveys place the number of newspaper journalists even lower – 25,000 in 2017, down from 52,000 in 2008. [59]

Many newspapers, especially those owned by large corporations and investment entities, such as hedge funds and private equity firms, have shed many more journalists. Since UNC did not have direct access to staffing levels at individual papers, we relied on information gleaned from news accounts, publicly available industry data and online research to estimate the number of newspapers still published in 2018 that have lost more than half their newsroom staffs since 2004. An estimated 1,000 newspapers – and as many as 1,500 – of the 7,200 newspapers still published in 2018 have drastically curtailed their distribution and their journalistic missions.

Ghost newspapers include both big-city metro papers, such as The Denver Post, which grabbed headlines with its journalists' revolt over the cutbacks in spring 2018, as well as state and regional dailies, such as The Wichita Eagle, that have dramatically cut their staffs and pulled back their news coverage of outlying areas in the region.

Many of the large metro dailies are owned by large investment groups —— hedge and private equity funds. These investment entities — such as New Media/GateHouse, Digital First and tronc/Tribune Publishing – have under their control some of the largest chains in the country. They employ the same formula for managing the hundreds of newspapers they purchased over the past decade at rock-bottom prices as they do for other properties they own and operate, such as financial institutions and real estate firms. That formula involves aggressive cost cutting, often paired with extensive financial restructuring, including bankruptcy. This invariably leads to short-staffed newsrooms that, of necessity, focus on quick-hit news stories instead of the more labor-intensive investigative and analytical pieces that are vitally important in providing a public service to the communities they cover.

At its peak in the mid 1990s, the New York Daily News circulated 2 million copies and often attracted national attention with its striking front-page headlines. The paper managed to retain its reputation for journalistic excellence, even as it has survived revolving-door owners, labor strikes, rapidly falling circulation and several rounds of layoffs in recent years. It has won 15 Pulitzer Prizes, the most recent coming just one year ago, when the paper received the Pulitzer Public Service Award for its coverage of the police department's widespread abuse of eviction rules.[60] In 2017, tronc, which has 77 papers and has significantly cut staff at the other large papers in its portfolio, acquired the Daily News for one dollar plus the assumption of liabilities. In August 2018, tronc laid off half of the remaining newsroom staff, leaving only 50 journalists to cover the five boroughs of largest city in the country. In a memo, company executives said the remaining staff would focus on "breaking news – especially in the areas of crime and civil justice."[61]

When the largest newspaper chain in the country, GateHouse, acquired The Providence Journal in 2014, layoffs started before the deal even closed. The Journal, known as "ProJo," bills itself as the oldest continuously published newspaper in the country. Throughout its 189-year history, the paper has won four Pulitzer Prizes, covering the state of Rhode Island and its capital city of Providence with more than 180,000 residents. In the 1990s, the paper boasted a circulation of 200,000 and a newsroom with more than 300 journalists. By July 2018, newsroom employment had been cut by 75 percent, bringing the staffing levels below 100. According to the NewsGuild-CWA, there were fewer than 20 reporters and columnists responsible for covering both state and city government. When asked by a former reporter why the Providence Journal no longer covered routine government meetings, Kirk Davis, CEO of GateHouse, replied that "covering routine government meetings doesn't automatically equate to earning 'watchdog status." [62]

A poll of guild representatives at 12 papers owned by Digital First Media, the third-largest newspaper chain in the country, indicated the company has slashed staff by more than twice the national average since 2012. At the Digital First-owned Denver Post, which received a Pulitzer Prize in 2013 for its coverage of the Aurora theater shooting, newsroom staffing has been reduced over the past six years from more than 180 to fewer than 70 journalists, who are responsible for covering a metro area with more than 2 million people. [63]

These cuts have also affected Digital First's smaller daily papers, sometimes more severely. The dozen or so Digital First papers in the Philadelphia area contributed more than $18 million toward the company's $160 million in profit in 2017 and led the company with a 30 percent profit margin. At the 23,000-circulation, 142-year-old Delaware County (Pennsylvania) Daily Times, the sole daily newspaper serving a county of more than 560,000 residents[64], newsroom staffing has been reduced from 100 to less than 30. In nearby Montgomery County, with a population of 800,000 residents, staffing at the 10,370-circulation Pottstown Mercury, which has received two Pulitzer Prizes for editorial writing and photography, has been cut from 73 in 2012 to 13.

DECLINE OF TOTAL U.S. NEWSROOM EMPLOYMENT: 2004-2017

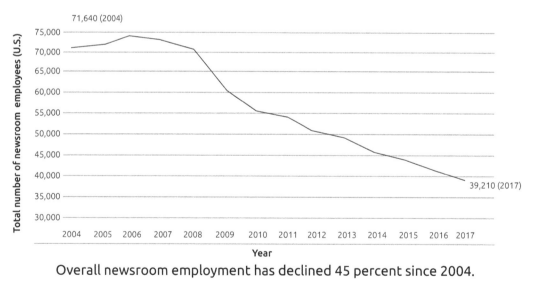

Overall newsroom employment has declined 45 percent since 2004.

SOURCE: Bureau of Labor Statistics

"I never thought it would get this bad," said Valerie Arkoosh, the chairwoman of the Montgomery Board of Commissioners. "There is virtually no coverage of school board meetings anymore. If [they] don't have the time to watch the stream [of the school board meetings], how do [they] know what's going on?" [65]

When metro, state and suburban papers – ranging from New York's Daily News to the Providence Journal and Pottstown Mercury – dramatically curtail coverage of local government meetings, citizens in a community are left without the information they need to make important decisions. At a 2018 meeting of county and city communicators from across North Carolina[66], participants bemoaned the lack of coverage of routine government meetings by local newspapers and worried that corruption is more likely to flourish at both the state and local levels. Other research has shown that governments tend to become less efficient when reporters do not shine a light on the actions of public officials.[67] Investigative journalism that wins prizes often results from reporting on routine, often tedious, town council or zoning board meetings, according to Howell Raines, former executive editor of The New York Times. Without aggressive boots-on-the-ground news coverage of these meetings by newspapers, "the news chain itself suffers," he said.[68]

BIGGER AND BIGGER THEY GROW

Consolidation of the newspaper industry, which places the ownership of many media properties into the hands of a few large corporations, shifts editorial and business decisions to people without a strong stake in the local communities where their papers are located.

The Largest Owners
The top 25 companies that own the most newspapers – control the fate of nearly one-third of all papers, up from 20 percent in 2004. This included two-thirds of all dailies – 812 – and almost a fourth of all weeklies – 1,376. The largest company, New Media/GateHouse, owns 451 newspapers in 34 states.

The Dizzying Turnover
The turnover in ownership has been dizzying. Roughly half of all newspapers in the country changed ownership over the past 15 years, some multiple times. Since 2014, most of the 1,200 papers sold have been either family-owned enterprises or small private regional chains. The most active purchasers of newspapers in recent years have been New Media/GateHouse, Adams Publishing and AIM Media. Over the past four years, these three chains have purchased nearly a third of the papers that were sold.

The Push Toward Regional Hubs
Economic pressures on the industry have prompted the largest companies to establish regional hubs, built around newspapers they already own. The majority of transactions in recent years involve a chain purchasing newspapers in adjacent markets. The purchaser then consolidates printing and back-office functions, as well as some sales and newsroom functions, significantly reducing the cost of operations.

The Surviving Independents
Fewer and fewer independently owned newspapers survive. As more and more family-owned newspapers sell to corporate chains, the number of independent weeklies is steadily declining. By 2018, fewer than one-third of the country's 5,829 weeklies with circulations under 15,000 were locally owned. Survival of the remaining independent newspapers depends in large measure on the ability of the publisher to generate new revenue to replace print revenue and to be very disciplined in managing costs.

THE LARGEST OWNERS

Even as the country loses papers, journalists and readers, consolidation in the industry continues apace. In 2018, the country's 7,100 papers were owned by only 2,600 firms. That is a decrease of 1,400 since 2004, and 400 since 2014 – or an average annual decrease of 100 newspaper companies a year. As the number of owners has decreased, consolidation – especially among the largest companies – has ballooned.

The largest 25 companies in 2018[69] owned nearly one-third of all papers, up from 20 percent in 2004. This included two-thirds of all dailies – 812 – and almost a fourth of all weeklies – 1,376. The largest 25 companies ranged in size from the 30 papers owned by Morris Multimedia to the 451 papers owned by New Media/GateHouse. The number of papers owned by the next largest group of owners – 26 through 50 – fell off dramatically. This group owned only 956 papers in total. Nevertheless, the largest 50 companies owned almost half – 45 percent – of all papers.

Ownership of the country's daily newspapers was concentrated among the largest 10 companies. Altogether, the largest 10 companies owned 1,500 papers, including almost half – 572 – of the country's 1,283 dailies. At the beginning of 2018, two of the 10 largest companies were publicly traded – Gannett and Lee Enterprises – and three were privately held – Adams Publishing, Ogden and Shaw.

LARGEST 25 COMPANIES IN 2018
RANKED BY NUMBER OF PAPERS OWNED

OWNER TYPE: PUBLIC   INVESTMENT   PRIVATE

Rank	Company	Total Papers	Daily Papers	Total Circ. (000s)	Daily Circ. (000s)
1	New Media/GateHouse	451	153	4,455	2,805
2	Gannett	216	107	4,301	3,249
3	Digital First Media	158	51	3,241	2,106
4	Adams Publishing Group	144	34	1,185	394
5	CNHI	114	73	1,006	707
6	Lee Enterprises	100	51	1,252	1,010
7	Ogden Newspapers	81	43	787	479
8	tronc/Tribune	77	17	2,462	1,705
9	BH Media Group	75	33	1,216	908
10	Shaw Media	71	10	385	111
11	Boone Newspapers	66	30	465	205
12	Hearst Corporation	66	22	1,586	924
13	Paxton Media Group	58	34	449	314
14	Landmark Media Enterprises	55	3	443	34
15	Community Media Group	51	13	270	72
16	AIM Media	50	25	450	271
17	McClatchy	49	30	1,782	1,509
18	Advance Publications	46	16	1,786	885
19	Rust Communications	44	18	251	141
20	News Media Corporation	43	3	188	15
21	Black Press Group	42	10	778	310
22	Forum Communications	38	11	298	133
23	Horizon Publications	33	22	147	101
24	Morris Multimedia	30	3	206	18
25	Trib Publications	30	0	95	0
	TOTALS	2,188	812	29,482	18,316

SOURCE: UNC Database

The other five large newspaper companies – New Media/Gatehouse, Digital First, CNHI/Raycom, tronc/Tribune and BH Media – were owned by investment entities, such as hedge and pension funds and private equity firms. Together, these five investment entities own 875 newspapers – or 60 percent of the 1,500 papers owned by the 10 largest owners. However, over the summer of 2018, both BH Media and CNHI announced plans to step back from newspaper ownership. The pension fund that owns CNHI announced plans to sell or close its 114 papers, and BH Media turned over day-to-day management of its 75 papers to Lee Enterprises. Additionally, tronc/Tribune is currently seeking new investors for its 77 papers. Therefore, the number of papers owned and operated by these large investment entities could shift significantly in the coming year.

Where the Largest 25 Companies Own Newspapers

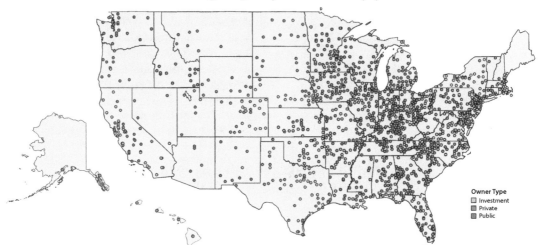

Owner Type
☐ Investment
■ Private
■ Public

The largest 25 newspaper chains own a third of all newspapers in the U.S., up from one-fifth in 2004. These large chains own two-thirds of all dailies.

THE DIZZYING TURNOVER

Roughly half of all newspapers in the country changed ownership over the past 15 years. In the years immediately after the 2008 recession, many of the transactions involved the purchase of large chains that were filing for bankruptcy, such as the Journal Register Company with 151 papers. However, since 2014, as the economy has picked up, most of the 1,200 papers sold have been either family-owned enterprises or small private regional chains. According to Dirks, Van Essen, Murray & April, there were 31 separate transactions involving daily newspapers and affiliated weeklies in 2017, the highest number of deals in a year since the turn of the 21st century. This year is on pace to exceed 2017. There have been 30 transactions through July 1, 2018. Newspapers sold over the last few years have gone for between two to five times annual earnings, down from historic highs of 13 times earnings before the 2008 recession. Therefore, despite the quickening pace, the dollar amount involved in these transactions remains far below the record levels reached in 2007.[70]

Most of the deals involved the sale of five or fewer papers. Even when large companies exited the market, their papers were sold to multiple owners in separate transactions. For example, Civitas, the seventh-largest newspaper chain in 2016, sold 86 of its papers to nine separate buyers. This included sales to such large privately held chains as AIM Media, which purchased 36; Adams, which purchased six; and Boone Newspapers, which bought three.[71]

Similarly, in 2016, 10/13 Communications, the 20th-largest newspaper chain, sold 42 of its papers to three separate buyers, Hearst in Houston, S.A.W. Advisors in Dallas, and Independent Newsmedia in Arizona.[72]

The most active purchasers of newspapers in recent years have been New Media/GateHouse, the country's largest chain with 451 papers; Gannett, the second largest with 216 papers; Adams Publishing, the fourth-largest with 144 papers; and AIM Media, the 16th- largest with 50 papers. Over the past four years, these four chains have

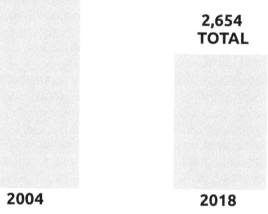

TOTAL NEWSPAPER OWNERS
2004, 2018

3,897 TOTAL

2004

2,654 TOTAL

2018

The total number of newspaper owners has declined 32 percent since 2004.

SOURCE: UNC Database

purchased 340 papers – or 30 percent of the papers that were sold. The privately held Adams, which was formed in 2013, and AIM, which was founded in 2012, are the new kids on the block, although their CEOs have extensive newspaper experience. Before founding these newspaper companies, the CEO of Adams was an investment banker specializing in media, and the CEO of AIM has held multiple executive positions in newspaper companies the last three decades, including CEO of Sun-Times Media.

The philosophy of the purchasers of newspapers is determined by their expectations about return on investment. The two largest investment firms – New Media/GateHouse and Digital First – actively manage their portfolio of properties, selling or closing underperforming papers. Since 2013, GateHouse has spent more than $1 billion purchasing 200 papers at an average of 4.1 times annual earnings[73], while also selling or closing nearly 50. In the same time period, Digital First has shed 46 papers while purchasing 29, including the Boston Herald in 2018. In contrast, both AIM and Adams say that they buy and hold. While both have recently purchased papers owned by private equity firms, both prefer family-owned enterprises, since those typically have strong ties to both local readers and advertisers. To date, neither Adams nor AIM has sold any of the almost 200 papers in their portfolios, though they have cut costs at the papers they purchase by centralizing printing, distribution and administrative functions. Both have a very lean corporate staff. In contrast to Gatehouse and Digital First, they both maintain a very low debt level and typically pay less than four times earnings. The lower purchase price leaves room for investment in the news and sales staff, they contend.[74]

The decision to sell a family-owned newspaper is an agonizing one, according to two owners who sold in 2016. Charles Broadwell, publisher of the 200-year-old Fayetteville Observer in Fayetteville, North Carolina, sold his 38,000-circulation paper to the GateHouse chain, ending four generations of family ownership. "Now, it's time to hand over the reins to a bigger company with national resources that, as a small family-owned entity, we just don't have," he said in announcing the sale. However, as GateHouse moved to quickly make cuts to newsroom staffing and replace Broadwell as publisher, he conceded the following year, "It was like walking around at my own funeral."[75]

Gregg Jones, CEO of Jones Media, received offers from a variety of other private chains as well as hedge-fund and private-equity chains when he decided to sell his fourth-generation family-owned company, which had a dozen small newspapers in Tennessee and western North Carolina. "I wanted to find the best buyers possible, and I thank God for the Adams family every day. . . . " Jones said in 2017. "The Adams family run their holdings efficiently. They are engaged in the community. They have no exit strategy." After purchasing Jones, Adams Publishing kept Jones on board as publisher of his own group of papers, plus appointed him as executive vice president responsible for almost all of its papers east of the Mississippi. Since then, Adams has added significantly to the papers it owns east of the Mississippi, purchasing 14 papers in North Carolina in two separate transactions and 13 in Florida.[76]

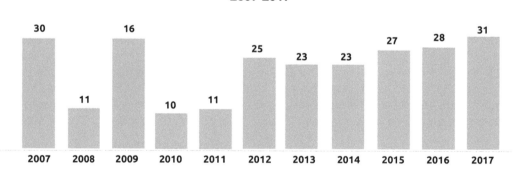

NUMBER OF ANNUAL NEWSPAPER TRANSACTIONS 2007-2017

2007	2008	2009	2010	2011	2012	2013	2014	2015	2016	2017
30	11	16	10	11	25	23	23	27	28	31

In 2017, transactions involving sales of daily newspapers were the highest recorded since 2000.

SOURCE: Dirks, Van Essen, Murray & April

THE PUSH TOWARD REGIONAL HUBS

The economics of the newspaper industry is driving newspaper sales across the country, forcing the sale of smaller, independent companies and prompting the largest companies to establish regional hubs, built around newspapers they already own. The majority of transactions in 2017 – 70 percent – involved a newspaper chain purchasing a single daily newspaper or a small cluster of dailies and weeklies in an adjacent market. The purchaser could then consolidate printing and back-office functions, as well as some sales and newsroom functions, thereby significantly cutting costs. "The sale to non-strategic buyers is becoming the exception rather than the rule." according to Dirks, Van Essen, Murray and April.[77]

For example, Hearst, which owns 66 papers, including more than 50 weekly papers, made strategic purchases in both Connecticut and Texas in 2017. The company purchased three dailies and eight weeklies from Digital First Media in Connecticut[78] to add to its existing portfolio of eight papers there. This brought Hearst's total weekly circulation in that state to more than 400,000. In Texas, it purchased more than 20 community newspapers located in the Houston suburbs from 10/13 Investments. These papers – including one daily in Conroe – were then converted into zoned editions of the 240,000-circulation Houston Chronicle, Texas' largest newspaper. This brought Hearst's total weekly circulation in the Houston area to more than 520,00 and its digital reach to more than 4 million.[79]

The holdings of the largest chains are concentrated in the eastern part of the country and along the Pacific coast. With the exception of GateHouse and Gannett, both of which own papers in 34 states, the other large companies have tended to focus their acquisitions on specific states. For example, all of the papers owned by AIM Media are located in four states. Likewise; all papers owned by Advance are in 11 states.[80]

Perhaps in no state has the move toward regional consolidation been more feverish than in Ohio. Since 2014, more than 30 percent of the state's papers have changed ownership. Five of the nation's largest newspaper chains –GateHouse, Gannett, Adams, AIM and Ogden – own nearly 120 papers in Ohio. GateHouse and AIM have been the most aggressive purchasers. AIM purchased 36 papers – including 16 small dailies – in the western and central part of the state from Civitas Media when it liquidated its Ohio holdings in 2017. It also owns eight papers in the adjacent state of Indiana.

While AIM and Adams focus on acquiring papers in small and mid-sized markets, GateHouse has increasingly turned its attention toward larger metro markets. In 2015, GateHouse, which owned a handful of papers in the towns in the northeastern part of Ohio, purchased 20 papers – including the Columbus Dispatch, with a circulation of 124,000 – from the family-owned and -operated Dix Communications. In 2018, it added to its collection of 50 papers in central and northeastern Ohio by purchasing the Akron Beacon Journal. "The Akron Beacon Journal is a great addition to our large Ohio footprint of properties," said CEO Michael Reed. "In addition to being a long-standing dominant source of award-winning journalism, its proximity to our properties in Wooster, Canton and Columbus is very exciting as we see many opportunities for growth."[81]

STAYING ALIVE:
THE SURVIVING INDEPENDENTS

As consolidation has increased, more and more small family-owned chains and independently operated newspapers are selling out to corporate chains. In 1997, half of all weeklies in the country were independent.[82] By 2018, fewer than one-third of the weeklies in the UNC database with circulation under 15,000 were independent or locally owned.

Survival of the remaining independent newspapers depends in large measure on the ability of the publisher to generate new revenue to replace print revenue. As profit margins on newspapers have dipped into the single digits in recent years, independent newspapers have very little room for error because they measure annual revenue in the low millions or hundreds of thousands of dollars. A slip-up in projecting revenue or expenses can lead to bankruptcy. Despite falling to record low levels, print advertising revenue still accounts for the majority of revenue and profit at most newspapers.

Complicating matters, in even the smallest markets, as much as 75 percent of the digital advertising dollars are going to Facebook and Google.[83] While some large national and metro papers have been able to diversify away from print advertising by raising the price they charge their readers, papers in smaller markets have little flexibility. Both print and digital consumers of news are especially price-sensitive in low-income markets. Even the wealthiest of the country's 3,143 counties have pockets of low-income neighborhoods or communities. Roughly two-thirds of counties where the remaining independents are located have overall poverty rates that exceed the national average. So publishers must be especially creative in coming up with ways to diversify their revenue, often looking outside their own geographic markets to find additional income.

Moore County, in the Sandhills region of eastern North Carolina, is home not only to the affluent resort and retirement communities of Pinehurst and Southern Pines, but also to a number of economically struggling communities that have lost their textile and furniture manufacturing base. As a result, the poverty rate for the county is 2

percentage points higher than the national average. The Pilot, a 100-year-old, family-owned community paper (with 13,000 circulation) published twice a week in Southern Pines, has aggressively sought new revenue from a variety of sources, even venturing outside Moore County to get it. Over the last several years, the company has introduced two state magazines – one focused on business and the other on the arts — three lifestyle magazines targeting North Carolina cities in different parts of the state, a series of electronic newsletters targeting subscribers and nonsubscribers, and three telephone directories for surrounding counties. In addition, the paper has established a digital media services agency that produces online and video content, and it has purchased an independent bookstore that hosts almost 200 author and community events a year. All the various ventures are ultimately aimed at building a strong sense of community among current and potential readers and advertisers of The Pilot. Currently only about a third of the revenue produced by the newspaper company comes from the newspaper itself. Because the company is able to spread the cost of operations over multiple publications and products, all the ventures are profitable.

In affluent Suffolk County at the tip end of New York's Long Island, Publisher Andrew Olsen is pursuing a similar diversification strategy with his three weekly newspapers, which have a combined circulation of 15,000. The oldest was founded 160 years ago. Until 2010, almost all revenue came from the print papers – with a disproportionate amount of advertising in the peak summer season – and a Shelter Island phone book that helped shore up the bottom line in the lean winter months when the tourists were gone. In a strategic pivot, Olsen began targeting lifestyle and digital products for growth. In 2013, the paper launched northforker. com, a digital news site covering food, drink, real estate and other activities in the area. Its online success inspired management in 2017 to create a print Northforker magazine, published 10 times a year. More and more, the Suffolk County papers are melding both their news and lifestyle coverage, as well as their print and digital distribution. Recent projects include an investigative piece about a murder, "Gone," which ran as a 10,000-word special section in the print papers and as a three-part documentary video, streamed online and screened at a local retirement village. "The Work We Do," a series of 300 video segments on blue-collar workers, is underwritten by local businesses. In addition, the papers are looking to partnerships that will allow their newsrooms to provide in-depth coverage of pressing issues. The East End News Project, organized by the editor, is a consortium of Suffolk County newspapers pooling their news resources to cover the opioid crisis. "We're a little mom-and-pop business," says Olsen. "So we have to blend creativity and financial discipline, and then ask, 'How are we going to get it done?'" [84]

FILLING THE LOCAL NEWS VOID

A 2011 Federal Communications Commission Report issued a clarion call for other media, both legacy and start-up, to fill the void in local news left when newspapers either closed or severely cut back their coverage of an area.[85] Many in the industry today are experimenting with new business models and new ways of covering local news. They range from journalists laid off by newspapers who have started digital sites to program directors at regional television stations and public access cable channels. However, most of these experiments are centered in and around our largest cities and metro areas. This means many areas of the country still are at risk of becoming news deserts.

Both legacy and start-up news outlets face unique, as well as shared, challenges in reaching residents in a community who are disenfranchised when a newspaper is closed. Legacy media must retrain journalists to engage viewers and convey news and information on a variety of platforms. Start-ups, which typically operate with lean business and editorial staffs, must work extra hard to become the go-to source for news and information. Both legacy and start-up franchises must develop new business models to pay for their new journalistic endeavors.

Local and Regional Television Newsrooms
As of 2017, local and regional television newsrooms employ more journalists than do newspapers, according to a broadcast industry survey. However, television still employs half the number of journalists who worked for newspapers a decade ago. This puts a premium on rethinking the production and dissemination of local television news. As viewership of the evening newscast declines, the most innovative stations are stepping up their digital efforts and experimenting with ways to revamp the delivery of on-air newscasts.

Public Access Cable Channels
Support for the nation's 3,000 or more public access cable channels is uneven. Some states have many such channels; other states have very few. Some channels are well-funded, others struggle to provide any programming. A handful of channels are moving beyond their original charter – that of providing residents in a community with a "video soapbox" for expressing diverse opinions and views – and beginning to offer news programming. This includes hosting interviews and roundtable discussions with candidates for local office, as well producing and airing documentaries on issues gripping the community, such as drug abuse.

Digital News Outlets
The most aggressive response to the loss of local newspapers has come from the more than 500 digital news outlets that span the country, covering everything from the environment to entertainment. Most have very lean staffs but attempt to provide coverage of important issues in a community. However, both the for-profit and nonprofit sites face significant funding challenges. Therefore, the vast majority of the online-only news sites are located in the larger, more affluent markets, where they are most likely to attract paying subscribers, advertisers or philanthropic support.

THE LEGACY BROADCASTERS
REACHING OUT TO NEW MARKETS AND AUDIENCES

In many ways, the nation's 1,700 licensed regional and local television stations seem the most obvious medium to fill the local news void. As of 2017, local and regional television newsrooms employ more journalists (27,100) than newspapers (25,000), according to a broadcast industry survey.[86] More people in the U.S. say they get their local news from television than from any other medium.[87] Also, unlike newspapers, which are facing declining profitability, local TV stations still operate with double-digit profit margins; half of the revenue for television stations with local news operations comes from the profitable evening newscasts.[88]

Once you delve into numbers, however, the challenges become apparent. Although television newsrooms employ more journalists than newspapers do, the total number of TV journalists is still half the number of newspaper journalists (52,000) employed in 2008.[89] In fact, the number of television journalists in 2017 actually declined by almost a thousand from the previous year. Similarly, while between a third and a half of people say they "often" get local news from television, viewership of the evening newscasts is declining and aging rapidly. According to the 2018 Pew Report, between 2016 and 2017 "the number of people who say they rely on television for their local news fell 9 percentage points, from 46 to 37 percent." Younger adults, under age 50, are much less likely to get their news from television than older adults.[90] Yet because the local newscast remains so profitable for local television stations, many stations have been reluctant to commit significant resources to online efforts to attract younger viewers. Only about 10 percent of most television station's revenue comes from digital, less than the newspaper industry average of 20 to 30 percent.[91]

In many ways, television stations have been a victim of their own success. As one general manager told the Knight Foundation, as long as profit margins remain high, there is less incentive to change. Even though TV stations have expanded the time allotted to news in many markets, various studies have found that the vast majority of those newscasts – often as much as 90 percent — revolve around "soft features," crime, weather, and sports." Additionally, the preponderance of stories covered by regional television stations are about issues and events that concern residents in the major metro market where they are located. When reporters do venture outside the metro area, they are most likely covering either weather events, such as tornadoes and hurricanes, or doing feature stories on people and activities, such as county fairs.[92]

A 2018 report by the Knight Foundation came back with four suggestions as to how television stations can step up their game and fill the news gap in many communities:[93]

1. **Focus on digital delivery of content, even though the return on investment isn't always there – yet.**

2. **Innovate, not just on the digital side but with on-air programming as well. Every TV newscast looks like all the other TV newscasts, but executives seem reluctant to try something new.**

3. **Drop the obsession with crime, carnage and mayhem. Focus on ways to connect with local communities through issues such as education, the economy and transportation.**

4. **Increase enterprise and investigative reporting. That requires hiring more experienced journalists and/or providing more newsroom training.**

The Knight Foundation found a number of local and regional television stations pushing forward, both innovating with the evening newscast and experimenting with digital platforms.

At KGMB-TV in Honolulu, newsroom leaders have given on-air reporters more time to dig deeper into nondeadline endeavors— rather than having to get stories done every day. KTVB in Boise, Idaho, is posting 360 videos on YouTube.

Roughly 20 percent of the television journalists hired in recent years have been digital-focused, as television stations attempt to beef up their websites, electronic newsletters and social media. "Right now, there might be too much emphasis on being quick and first, and that gets in the way of a lot of quality digital storytelling," Autumn Hand, digital video and syndication manager at The E.W.

Scripps Co., told Knight. However, Ellen Crooke, vice president of news at Tegna Media, said, "Some of our most innovative projects have involved digital episodic content that is digital first. . . . With digital first, we reach more people than just running a piece on Thursday night. We'll have millions of page views. We've changed lives and changed laws; we've reached a younger audience." Tegna's efforts include projects exploring suicides among military veterans, heroin addiction and sex trafficking.[94]

In Raleigh, North Carolina, WRAL, the state's oldest licensed station, has stressed beat reporting and specialized expertise. News Director Rick Gall said WRAL is attempting to take on more of the role local papers once played in informing communities throughout the state. It is investing "in specialty reporting, especially on the web . . . in education, business, high school sports, government coverage. We produce web-only or primarily web content on all these areas."[95] The WRAL.com education reporter, for example, recently partnered with a reporter at a nonprofit startup that covers educational issues to produce a series on a new program designed to give poor-performing schools more latitude in designing curriculum. A WRAL.com newsletter features a roundup of editorials published in newspapers throughout the state and country on issues and topics of concern to North Carolinians. WRAL also publishes its own editorials on the website.

WRAL's website has almost 50 percent more daily visitors than the Raleigh News & Observer's and almost three times the number of page views, according to recent tracking.[96] The Knight Foundation report found that while newspaper sites in the very largest markets attract the most viewers, TV websites in most markets outside the top 25 markets attract the most viewers. As several news directors pointed out, television stations should hold an edge over newspapers on the web since they know how to produce compelling video of breaking news events. But if television stations are going to meaningfully fill the news gap, broadcast journalists need to learn how to use that video experience and knowledge to engage a younger audience, as well as residents in rural areas without dependable internet.

THE PUBLIC ACCESS CHANNELS
PROVIDING NEWS OR DIVERSITY OF VIEWS

STATES WITH THE MOST
PUBLIC ACCESS CHANNELS (PEGs)
2018

State	Number of Public Access Channels
Massachusetts	106
California	38
New York	21
Michigan	16
Vermont	16
Minnesota	15
Ohio	15
Connecticut	14
New Hampshire	12
Maryland	10

Note: This ranking solely reflects members of the Alliance for Community Media
SOURCE: Alliance for Community Media

The 1984 Cable Act[97] gave communities throughout the country the ability to require cable operators to set aside funds for public access channels known as "PEGs," or "public, educational, and governmental access channels." These channels were originally envisioned as "the video equivalent of the speaker's soapbox" that would provide all residents in a community the chance to have their voices heard. In recent years, as more and more newspapers have closed, community activists, as well as industry leaders, have begun to re-evaluate and debate the mission of the estimated 3,000 to 5,000 public access channels in the country.[98] Is their core purpose still free and diverse expression from community members? Or are these channels capable of filling the news and information gap left when a local newspaper dies?

Almost 35 years after the Cable Act was passed by Congress, local support for the public access channels is uneven. Depending on the community, the local government, the state or even the local cable company can oversee a public access channel and determine both its funding and programming.

"In some places, the [public access channels] are pretty well-situated to be able to respond to the local needs," says Mike Wassenaar, CEO of the Alliance for Community Media (ACM)), which lobbies on behalf of PEGS.[99] "In other cases, they need a lot of help." There are 363 public access channels in 42 states that are members of the ACM. These channels offer a variety of programming. Some record local governmental meetings, others attempt to capture the personal video histories of local residents, and still others offer educational programming. [100]

Some states have dozens of PEGs; other states have only a handful. Massachusetts has about 230 outlets serving the state's 16 million residents; half these outlets belong to ACM. On the other hand, Georgia, which has a population of 10 million and 28 counties without a local newspaper, has only two public access channels that belong to ACM. Many PEGs are in very small communities, but Wassenaar points out that with funding, as well as commitment by the local franchising authority, there is the potential for these channels to provide news coverage of communities that may not have any other local news outlet. "Depending on the state you're in, you either have a lot of resources, or you have no resources," Wassenaar said. In general, the New England states have more active public access channels. Vermont, which has only 600,000 residents, has 25 such channels; 16 belong to ACM.

In New York City's outer boroughs of Brooklyn and the Bronx, two public access channels are demonstrating how to fill the local news gap. In late June, New Yorkers were preparing to vote on the two Democratic candidates for the state's 14th Congressional District, which covers parts of the Bronx and Queens. Newcomer Alexandria Ocasio-Cortez was challenging longtime incumbent representative Joe Crowley. At Lehman College, part of the City University of New York system, BronxNet did its best to hold the candidates accountable. About a week before the election, the PEG channel held 10-minute "In the District Vote 2018" interviews with Ocasio-Cortez and Crowley. The clips were aired on BronxNet, posted on the PEG's website and uploaded to YouTube. Phil Lane, director of finance and business affairs, sees public affairs content as an important component of BronxNet's mission. "We do local debates," Lane said. "We do local city council, local Congress, local state assembly, everything across the board. . .. So there's definitely an opportunity to fill [information] voids." The channel also collaborates with community newspapers such as the Riverdale Press and the Norwood News to host "Meet The Press"-style roundtables.[101]

In Brooklyn, Executive Producer Aziz Isham of BRIC-TV, a "nonprofit community channel and digital network," attempts to fulfill two goals – providing local news while also giving local residents a chance to make their voices and positions known. Initiatives range from a hard-hitting documentary on how the opioid crisis is affecting the borough's Hasidic community to Brooklyn Free Speech, a "public access initiative" that provides education to New Yorkers on how to use their technology to make their voices heard. "There's something valuable about having news directors, or the equivalent, on staff [to] provide some sort of editorial guidance and training," Isham said. "But I also think it's really valuable and really important that we're engaging passionate amateurs and people from the community who want to tell stories."[102]

DIGITAL START UPS
THE NEW KIDS ON THE BLOCK

The most aggressive response to the loss of local newspapers has come from the several hundred digital news outlets that span the country, most of them started in the past decade by journalists. The Local Independent Online News (LION) association counts 525 "local" digital outlets, a collection of both for-profit and nonprofit sites. About two-thirds provide residents in their communities a mix of coverage on government, politics, business, sports and lifestyle features – similar to the range of topics in community newspapers. The others either provide coverage of state and regional issues, such as health care and the environment, or focus on niche topics, ranging from tourism to parenting and entertainment. [103]

Despite the enthusiasm with which digital sites have been established, a 2015 survey by the Los Angeles Times found that one in four failed. A 2016 analysis of 153 online news sites in 56 markets, sponsored by the Knight Foundation, concluded that only one in five of these news sites attracted enough visitors and funding to be self-sufficient. A quarter of the "self-sufficient" sites were nonprofit, and two-thirds were located in the seven largest metro areas in the country. [104]

UNC analysis of the local news sites identified by LION revealed a similar pattern. Ninety percent are clustered around metro areas, in cities or adjacent suburbs, which offer more funding possibilities for start-ups. Most are located in affluent communities, where residents have multiple media options and tend to vote Democratic. This is in contrast to the rural, fly-over counties that have lost newspapers, which tend to be poorer, have very few media options and vote Republican.

Roughly 400 local news sites have been started in communities that lost a newspaper over the past decade and a half. However, only two of the outlets are in the 171 counties in the U.S. that have no newspaper.

One is a for-a profit endeavor, the Orleans Hub, in Orleans County, New York, which borders Lake

WHERE DIGITAL NEWS SITES ARE FILLING THE VOID

While the U.S has lost almost 1,800 newspapers, only about 500 local or state digital news sites have filled the void.
Most of these sites are in metro areas.
Source: Local Independent Online News (LION) Publishers

Ontario and has 43,000 residents. The county's last surviving paper, The Medina Journal, closed in 2014. The Hub, which covers typical community news, ranging from high school sports to local crime, was started by the owner of the nearby Lake County Pennysaver. She paid the editor with profits from the Pennysaver until there was enough revenue from online advertising to make the Hub site self-sufficient. The Hub currently has 100 digital advertisers.[105]

The other site, KY Forward, founded in 2018, is nonprofit and covers the region including Kenton County, Kentucky, which is a suburb of Cincinnati and has 165,000 residents. In 2008, E. W. Scripps shuttered both the Cincinnati Post in Ohio and its sister paper, the Kentucky Post, located in the county seat of Covington. KY Forward is part of the outreach of the Kentucky Center for Public Service Journalism, which produces in-depth stories on education, government and health, and covers state news, including business and sports. It contracts with professional journalists and collaborates with journalism classes and students. The Center is funded by grants from individuals, foundations and organizations, including Toyota and Northern Kentucky University.[106]

For-profit and nonprofit sites face many of the same funding challenges. Both must seek diverse sources of funding right out of the gate.

For-profit entities must find advertisers, sponsors, subscribers and others who will either pay to access their content or underwrite the cost of producing the stories on their sites. For that reason, they tend to offer a diverse menu of news – including entertainment, business and sports coverage that tends to attract both readers, sponsors and advertisers. Andaiye Taylor, founder of Brick City Live in Newark, discovered through trial and error that the site's calendar of events offered the key to financial success. Organizers of events pay extra in order for their ads to stand out on the calendar. Additionally, Brick City Live Tickets offers promoters of events the opportunity to sell tickets to users of the news site at a reduced fee.

In contrast, Honolulu Civil Beat in Hawaii, which focuses on producing enterprise and investigative journalism, launched as a for-profit subscription site in 2010 with startup support from eBay founder Pierre Omidyar. In June 2016, it converted to a nonprofit. "People who were reluctant to buy a subscription [to a for-profit site] were happy to donate [to a nonprofit]," said editor and general manager Patti Epler. "Many saw their donations as sending a signal to policymakers that we were doing important work and they wanted it to continue."

Nonprofits rely disproportionately on donations from individuals or grants from philanthropic organizations. The average nonprofit receives only 20 percent of its funds from individuals and about 60 percent from foundation grants made by a small pool of philanthropic foundations.[107] Even worse, the foundation grants often are made for a specific period (three to five years), and distributed across hundreds of organizations, in an attempt to seed innovation. Only two-thirds of the $1.8 billion in grants made to support journalism between 2010 and 2015 went to nonprofit news-gathering organizations, with a third of that amount given to just 25 public media stations in 10 states. The rest went toward research and technology development, and to programs at universities in some of the nation's largest cities. Local and state news nonprofits received only 5 percent of the total pool.[108]

There are 179 members of the Institute for Nonprofit News. A survey in 2012 found that two-thirds of its members – such as ProPublica, the Marshall Project and the Texas Tribune – focused on international, national and state news. All but two of the hyperlocal sites were in large cities. VTDigger in Vermont and Flint Beat in Michigan, both founded by veteran journalists, are a study in contrasts and illustrate the challenges and possibilities confronting nonprofit startups.

VTDigger launched in 2009 with a single employee, who had been laid off from the Rutland Herald, and $12,500 in startup funds from three Vermont foundations.[109] It has grown to be a 19-employee operation, including 15 journalists, with an annual budget of $1.2 million.[110] The key to the organization's success has been the significant funding it received from wealthy donors as well as regional businesses and foundations, such as Ben and Jerry's, the Vermont Country Store and the Vermont Community Foundation (a group of more than a hundred funds and foundations created by Vermonters to "serve their charitable goals").[111] The site in 2018 has nearly 245,000 unique visitors monthly who look to VTDigger to produce regional stories on everything from state legislative issues to a series on alleged fraud at Vermont's Jay Peak ski resort. Half of the VTDigger readers live outside Vermont; 57 percent don't subscribe to a print newspaper. Eighty-six percent of the site's readers have a college degree, and another 69 percent have household earnings above $60,000. By 2022, VTDigger expects to have a $3 million budget and double the number of current readers.[112]

In Flint, Michigan, where more than 40 percent of residents live in poverty[113], Flint Beat faces a different prospect. In the wake of the city's contaminated water crisis, journalist and Flint-area native Jiquanda Johnson left the newsroom at MLive Media Group, which produces the daily 41,000-circulation Flint Journal, to start the site in 2017. "I stepped out on journalistic faith to give the Flint community the news and coverage they deserve," Johnson says on the site.[114] "We have a community journalism approach where we cover all things Flint. The website features news from city hall, neighborhoods and local news, as well as information on the Flint water crisis." In 2017, Flint Beat brought in less than $5,000 in advertising. A crowdfunding initiative launched before the site went live raised just $1,235 of its $25,000 goal.[115] In 2018, the site received $5,000 from the Solutions Journalism Network and another $7,500 from a LION local advertising mentorship program. Johnson has had to take a marketing position to keep Flint Beat afloat.[116] She also faces the challenge of engaging community residents. More than 40 percent of households in Flint don't have an internet subscription, compared with 17 percent nationally.[117] Johnson has sought to improve news literacy in Flint by working with local agencies to open a community media center that will train high school students as journalists.

"You have to, in some cases, develop the habit of local news. If local news coverage doesn't exist, people don't know that they need it or want it," said Matt DeRienzo, executive director of LION.[118] "If you haven't seen an article about a school board's deliberation over a bond issue, ever, why do you need to know that's something worth reading or even caring about? And that's really bedrock democracy stuff, too." The people of Flint "are not voiceless; they just don't have a platform," Johnson said. "Flint Beat is that platform." Now Flint Beat just needs to find the funding to amplify that voice.[119]

Because of the variety of issues confronting start-up news sites, a 2018 study by the Knight Foundation concluded, "The bottom line is that the primary suppliers of local news online remain newspapers (primarily core city dailies) and television stations (primarily the big four network affiliates). . .. The few successful exceptions in smaller markets prove that stand-alone online news sites are possible, but the numbers strongly suggest that we're a long way from stand-alone news websites as a major factor in local news."[120]

THE CHALLENGES AND OPPORTUNITIES THAT REMAIN

Our sense of community and our trust in democracy at all levels suffer when journalism is lost or diminished. In an age of fake news and divisive national politics, the fate of communities across the country, and of grassroots democracy itself, is linked – more than ever – to the vitality of local journalism. Local newspapers have historically been a "tie that binds" people in a community. Through the stories they publish, local newspapers help us "understand how we are related to people we may not know we are related to." They also educate us, providing us with information to guide important decisions that will affect the quality of our own lives, as well as those of future generations. An entire community – even nonvoters – benefits when voters make informed decisions about local candidates and policies.[121]

Given the tenuous financial situation confronting local newspapers today, many will not survive. The stakes are high, not just for the communities that have lost newspapers — or are living with the threat of losing a local newspaper – but also for the entire country. It will take a concerted and coordinated effort among numerous interested parties – concerned citizens, community activists, philanthropists, universities, classroom educators, policy makers, journalists and various industry groups – to address the business and journalistic challenges that must still be surmounted if we are to have a robust news ecosystem.

While the business model that sustained local journalism for two centuries has been demolished in less than two decades, many entrepreneurs are experimenting with for-profit and nonprofit ventures in hopes of filling the void when a local newspaper closes or reviving the fortunes of a struggling organization. In cities, hundreds of digital sites, public access channels and regional television stations are trying to reach and engage new audiences on new platforms. In small and mid-sized markets, entrepreneurs with extensive media experience, such as the CEOs of AIM and Adams Publishing are seizing the opportunity to purchase family-owned newspapers at record low prices and build privately owned regional chains that are different – in cost structure, vision and mission – from their 20th century publicly traded predecessors, such as Gannett and the Tribune Co. Other publishers of independent, family-owned papers in small and mid-sized markets – such as The Pilot in Southern Pines or the Suffolk County weekly papers in Long Island – are choosing to double down on their investment in their own communities, even as they experiment with new business models to accommodate the preferences of readers and advertisers in the digital age.

Recent research has identified five lessons that are relevant to any local news organization hoping to survive and thrive in the digital age. Local news organizations that are successfully adapting: [122]

Invest in their human capital – their journalists and sales departments.
Human capital is what sets them apart and makes them relevant to residents and businesses in their community.

Tie their strategy and business model to the specific needs of the communities they serve.
This means that, instead of one business model that works for most news organizations, as has historically been the case, there will be many.

Diversify their sources of revenue, moving away from print advertising.
However, in most small and mid-sized markets, the majority of revenue will most likely come from advertisers and sponsors. Since advertisers follow audiences, news organizations need to follow the technology and follow their customers if they are going to follow the money. Therefore, successful news

organizations build services and products that will attract dollars from local advertisers and engage local residents on a variety of platforms and venues.

Know when to compete, and when to collaborate, on both journalistic and business ventures. Partnerships may ultimately determine the ability of independent and nonprofit organizations to survive, since they are stronger together.

Have a strategy in place for transforming at least a third of their business model every five years. Their leaders establish five-year financial goals (for costs, revenue and profitability), and then identify and prioritize initiatives most likely to lead to long-term profitability and sustainability, even if that means lower profit today.

For the most part, local news outlets that have pursued strategies based on the specific needs of their communities have begun to reap the fruits of their investments. The leaders of these news organizations possess both journalistic civic responsibility, as well as the business savvy to discard old business models, even as they are experimenting with and creating new ones.

But there are many forces that remain beyond the control of individual publishers, news directors, editors and founders of local news organizations – especially those in communities that are struggling economically. If we are to thwart the rise of news deserts, interested parties – especially community activists, politicians, universities, philanthropic organizations and government agencies – will need to coordinate and collaborate around these three major initiatives:

Increased public and nonprofit funding for journalistic organizations located in communities at risk of becoming news deserts: Economists call public service journalism a "public good" because the information conveyed through news stories helps guide decision-making at all levels of our society.[123] Theoretically, at least, informed citizens and public officials craft better policies that benefit the entire community., In the 20th century, print newspaper advertising, which often accounted for 80 percent or more of revenue, essentially underwrote the journalism in most communities. Now that print advertising has evaporated, we have what economists call a "market failure," especially in low-income, isolated communities. There is simply not enough digital or print revenue in some rural communities or struggling inner-city neighborhoods and suburbs to pay for public service journalism.

Therefore, some scholars are arguing that instead of being considered a "public good," journalism should be considered a "merit good," a product or service that should be provided free of charge by the government, regardless of an individual's ability to pay. This suggests the need for more federal government funding of public media, such as NPR and PBS, as well as a renewed commitment by those national broadcasting networks to cover communities in danger of becoming news deserts. Such funding, paid for by tax dollars, can also come from both state and local governments. In 2018, the New Jersey state legislature, for example, set aside $5 million for a Civic Information Consortium that would award grants to news organizations that cover neglected communities. Similarly, some of the public access cable channels (PEGs) receive support from their local municipalities that allows them to broadcast or stream governmental meetings.[124]

Lacking government support, the responsibility for filling the journalistic void when a newspaper dies invariably falls to various philanthropic organizations and community foundations. The small amount of philanthropic funding supporting journalistic endeavors in recent years does not begin to replace the billions of print dollars that have evaporated. Even worse, only 5 percent of the $1.8 billion distributed by 6,500 philanthropic foundations between 2010 and 2015 went to state and local news organizations. As a result, there are very few nonprofit organizations covering the concerns of economically struggling "flyover regions" of the country. Since there is little coordination among the various foundations and philanthropic organizations funding journalistic endeavors, a preponderance goes to nonprofit news organizations located in major metro areas that cover national or international issues. [125]

Therefore, there is a compelling need for philanthropic foundations, community activists, local government, concerned citizens and potential founders of nonprofit news organizations to work together from the beginning to identify communities most lacking coverage and the funding needed to sustain a start-up news organization in those communities. Additionally, existing nonprofit organizations that are currently receiving the majority of philanthropic funding need to be charged with doing more to collaborate with both for-profit and nonprofit news organizations in the often-ignored flyover regions.

Rethinking policies and programs that will reinvigorate the for-profit journalism model. While philanthropic and governmental funding can be effective in targeted situations, long-term the country needs to develop for-profit models, in order to ensure a robust news environment, as well as the social and economic health of the thousands of small and mid-sized communities where they are located. For-profit newspapers have historically played an important role in encouraging local and regional economic development, as the advertisements in their pages have brought consumers and local businesses together. In return, local business paid for the ads that supported the news-gathering operation. Structural changes have altered that symbiotic relationship, and newspapers now find the business odds stacked against them as they attempt to move from a print business model to a digital one.

In even the smallest markets, Facebook and Google now receive as much as 75 percent of all digital advertising dollars.[126] This leaves every news organization in a community – legacy and start-up – fighting over the remaining 25 percent, a zero-sum game. Whatever portion a news outlet manages to eke out, it is not enough to sustain local public service journalism over the long term. Media scholars and industry professionals are expressing growing alarm that Facebook's and Google's dominance is preventing newspapers from successfully transitioning from print to a profitable digital business model. The News Media Alliance, a national association of 2,000 news outlets, is lobbying for a change to antitrust laws that would allow newspapers to collectively bargain with tech and social media giants for stronger intellectual property protections and a bigger share of revenue. A growing number of scholars are proposing that these digital giants be held to the same standards as news organizations, subject to libel and privacy laws. Rupert Murdoch has proposed that Facebook and Google pay news organizations for the journalism on their platforms. [127]

In the wake of their slip-ups during the 2016 election – and their slow response acknowledging the problems – both Google and Facebook are also facing increased scrutiny here and abroad from Congress and various regulatory agencies, and calls in some quarters for these giants to be regulated as "public utilities." Given the attitude of the current administration, it is unlikely that there will be a dramatic rethinking of antitrust laws and FCC regulations in the coming months. But, even if some of these policy proposals are enacted, they likely would not make a significant difference in the long-term financial health of newspapers in small and mid-sized markets. Unlike the large national and metro papers, small-market newspapers simply do not have the reach and scale to reap much financially from an ad "revenue-sharing" arrangement or a pay-for-use of news articles.

Google and Facebook recorded earnings before interest and taxes of $26 billion and $16 billion, respectively, in 2017. Their executives continue to insist they are a "platform" or "technology company" – not a "media company." But, as a consequence of their companies' role in disseminating fake news, there is a growing realization – among the public, the business community and politicians – that the fate of these "tech companies" is tied in many ways to the sustainability of news organizations in thousands of communities around the country. So far, the two tech companies have only set aside a small fraction of their profits to experiment with new business models for news organizations. Much more of a financial commitment is needed from the digital giants. [128]

Additionally, it is imperative that industry organizations, universities, government agencies, newspaper owners, elected officials and community activists redouble efforts to find new and creative ways for local news organizations to thrive financially in the digital age – especially those in small and mid-sized markets. At the 2018 annual shareholder meeting of Berkshire Hathaway, Warren Buffett admitted that his company's recent investment in a chain of newspapers in mid-sized communities in the South and Midwest had fallen short of expectations. He predicted a grim future for all but a handful of the country's largest newspapers, such as The New York Times, which has successfully looked to its subscribers to pay more and replace a significant portion of lost advertising revenue. If newspapers in the digital age must rely primarily on subscriber revenue to fund their newsrooms, however, very shortly, only the largest and most affluent communities in the country will have for-profit news organizations.

Encouraging a renewed emphasis on civic and media literacy. For our democracy to function at all levels, we need to be able to easily access reliable news and information. We then need to know what we can do to act on that information. Testifying before the Knight Commission on Trust, Media and Democracy, Michael Cormack Jr., CEO of the nonprofit Barksdale Reading Institute in Mississippi, asserted that democracy is hampered when a large percentage of our population is not "fully" literate. Being literate, he argued, is about more than simply comprehending the meaning of words; it is about the ability to analyze arguments and identify what is supported by facts.[129]

The run-up to the 2016 election taught us how quickly false and fake news can spread in the digital era – and that there was little recourse for correcting misinformation. The McCormick Foundation, among others, has noted that "a growing sector of the U.S. population" does not distinguish between news sources and that "the 24/7 news cycles and digital advances" compound the problem. There has been renewed interest in educating high school and college students on the importance of media literacy. Others in the industry are advocating for expansion of those programs to reach adults, especially those in at-risk communities such as Flint, Michigan, where the founder of the nonprofit news site Flint Beat has struggled to engage the residents in a community still reeling from a host of issues resulting from the pollution of its water system.

News deserts arise not only when local journalistic organizations fail financially, but also when residents in a community do not know how to access and use the information that a news outlet provides. Researchers have noted a strong correlation between news deserts and food deserts, as well as low voter turnout in economically struggling communities. "If you haven't seen an article about a school board's deliberation over a bond issue, ever, why do you need to know that's something worth reading, or even caring about?" asks Matt DeRienzo, executive director of the Local Independent Online News association.[130] Historically, strong local newspapers have informed communities about important issues and built social identity, which, in turn, encourages political activism. That is why community organizations (such as libraries and civic clubs), local government agencies and elected officials, news organizations and educators from early childhood through college need to work together to foster civic and media literacy programs that stress the important relationship between strong local journalism and a healthy community.

The fates of communities and local news organizations are intrinsically linked — socially, politically and economically. Trust and credibility suffer when local news media are lost or diminished. We need to make sure that whatever replaces the 20th century version of local newspapers serves the same community-building functions. If we can figure out how to craft and implement sustainable news business models in our smallest, poorest markets, we can then empower journalistic entrepreneurs to revive and restore trust in media from the grassroots level up, in whatever form – print, broadcast or digital. [131]

Senior Researcher/Writer Erinn Whitaker and Research Assistant Alex Dixon compiled data and provided much of the analysis in this report. Both are staff researchers with the Center for Innovation and Sustainability in Local Media in the School of Media and Journalism at the University of North Carolina at Chapel Hill.

CITATIONS

1   The Rise of a New Media Baron and the Emerging Threat of News Deserts, The Center for Innovation and Sustainability in Local Media, (University of North Carolina at Chapel Hill, 2016) See also: Penelope Muse Abernathy, Saving Community Journalism: The Path to Profitability, (Chapel Hill: UNC Press, 2014)

2   Steven Waldman, The Information Needs of Communities: The changing media landscape in a broadband age, Federal Communications Commission, July 2011, https://transition.fcc.gov/osp/inc-report/The_Information_ Needs_of_Communities.pdf See also: Manpower Development Corporation, The Building Blocks of Community Development, MDC Inc., 2002;

3   This measure includes US county and county equivalents as defined by the United States Census Bureau. For example, this includes 29 boroughs and census areas in Alaska. https://www.census.gov/geographies/reference-files.html

4   Rural and nonrural classification is derived from United States Department of Agriculture's Rural-Urban Continuum Codes (RUCC) definition of metro and nonmetro. Metro counties include counties that fall within RUCC 1-3 while nonmetro counties fall within RUCC 4-9. https://www.ers.usda.gov/data-products/rural-urban-continuum-codes/documentation/.

5   United States Census Bureau: Pryor Creek, Oklahoma, 2017, https://www.census.gov/quickfacts/pryorcreekcityoklahoma

6   William W. Savage III, "Pryor Daily Times closes, locals 'stunned' by loss of online archives," nondoc.com, May 10, 2017, https://nondoc.com/2017/05/10/pryor-daily-times-closes-locals/

7   United States Census Bureau: Gridley, California, 2017, https://www.census.gov/quickfacts/gridleycitycalifornia

8   Risa Johnson, "With one day's notice, Gridley Herald staff prints final issue, closes its doors" Chico Enterprise-Record, August 31, 2018, https://www.chicoer.com/2018/08/31/with-one-days-notice-gridley-herald-staff-prints-final-issue-closes-its-doors/

9   Penelope Muse Abernathy, Saving Community Journalism: The Path to Profitability, (Chapel Hill: UNC Press, 2014)

10   Judith Miller, "News Deserts: No News Is Bad News," Urban Policy 2018, Manhattan Institute, October 2, 2018, https://www.manhattan-institute.org/html/urban-policy-2018-news-deserts-no-news-bad-news-11510.html

11   Jim Conaghan, Interview with Penny Abernathy discussing digital and print readership, May 02, 2016

12   "2016 Broadband Progress Report," Federal Communications Commission, January 29, 2016, https://www.fcc.gov/reports-research/reports/broadband-progress-reports/2016-broadband-progress-report

13   Marissa Lang, "Oakland loses Tribune, with paper folded into new East Bay Times," San Francisco Chronicle, March 1, 2016, https://www.sfgate.com/business/article/Bay-Area-News-Group-consolidates-newspapers-6863720.php See also: circulation from Alliance for Audited Media

14   Keoki Kerr, "Merged Honolulu Star-Advertiser Begins June 7," KITV, May 12, 2010, https://web.archive.org/web/20120121154944/http:/www.kitv.com/news/23536804/detail.html

15   Helen Branswell, "As towns lose their newspapers, disease detectives are left to fly blind," STAT, March 20, 2018, https://www.statnews.com/2018/03/20/news-deserts-infectious-disease/

16   2018 UNC Database, Center for Innovation and Sustainability in Local Media

17   Income and Poverty in the United States: 2016, United States Census Bureau, September 12, 2017, https://www.census.gov/library/publications/2017/demo/p60-259.html

18   News desert counties were cross-referenced with the USDA's Food Access Research Atlas to identify counties that have tracts classified as low-income and low-access to food from a supermarket. https://www.ers.usda.gov/data/fooddesert/

19   James Hamilton and Fiona Morgan, "Poor Information: How Economics Affects the Information Lives of Low Income Individuals," International Journal of Communication 12, 2018, 2832-2850.

20   States were grouped into regions according to the following classifications:
Pacific: AK, CA, HI, OR, WA; Mountain: AZ, CO, ID, MT, NV, NM, UT, WY; Midwest: IL, IN, MI, OH, WI, IA, KS, MN, MO, NE, ND, SD; Mid-Atlantic: NJ, NY, PA; South: DE, DC, FL, GA, MD, NC, SC, VA, WV, AL, KY, MS, TN, AR, LA, OK, TX; New England: CT, ME, MA, NH, RI, VT

21   "Baldwin City Signal Ending Publication With Current Edition," Baldwin City Signal, December 30, 2015, http://signal.baldwincity.com/news/2015/dec/30/baldwin-city-signal-cease-publication-dec-31/

22   Steven Smethers, "Silent 'Signal': Baldwin City adjusts to life without a newspaper." Kansas State University presentation, April 11, 2018

23   Rick Brand, "Suffolk Life Publisher David Wilmott dead at 71,"Newsday, August 10, 2009, https://www.newsday.com/long-island/obituaries/suffolk-life-publisher-david-willmott-dead-at-71-1.1361055

24   Free circulation from Beth Young, "Suffolk Life goes out of business after 47 years," Southampton Press, June 18, 2008, http://www.27east.com/news/article.cfm/Southampton/150909/Suffolk-Life-goes-out-of-business-after-47-years
See also: paid circulation from Editor and Publisher, International Year Book, 2007

25   Andrea Aurichio, "David J. Willmott, Sr., Suffolk Life Newspapers Publisher, Dies At 71," Hamptons Online Media, http://www.hamptons.com/Community/Obituaries/8606/David-J.-Willmott-Sr.-Suffolk-Life-Newspapers.html#.W6JJbEVKjUL

26   Preethi Dumpala, "The Year the Newspaper Died," Business Insider, July 4, 2009, https://www.businessinsider.com/the-death-of-the-american-newspaper-2009-7

27   United States Census Bureau: Wheeling village, Illinois, 2017, https://www.census.gov/quickfacts/fact/table/wheelingvillageillinois/PST045217

28   Larry Green, "A Note to Our Readers," Wheeling Countryside, January 15, 2009

29   Jon Chesto, "GateHouse Media's growth bucks the trend," Boston Globe, March 11, 2015, https://www. bostonglobe.com/business/2015/03/10/meet-newspaper-industry-biggest-deal-maker/vV6D7uqAo7ssLPaIPk58oL/ story.html

30   Paige Pfleger, "When The Local Paper Closes, Where Does The Community Turn?" National Public Radio, June 21, 2015, https://www.npr.org/2015/06/21/415199073/when-the-local-paper-closes-where-does-the-community-turn

31   "2016 Broadband Progress Report," Federal Communications Commission, January 29, 2016, https://www.fcc.gov/reports-research/reports/broadband-progress-reports/2016-broadband-progress-report

32   Danielle Kurtzleben, "Rural Voters Helped Trump Win The Election. Here's How," National Public Radio, November 14, 2016, https://www.npr.org/2016/11/14/501737150/rural-voters-played-a-big-part-in-helping-trump-defeat-clinton

33   "About the Lime Springs Herald," Lime Springs Herald, https://limespringsherald.wordpress.com/about/

34   Marcie Klomp, "Lime Springs school to close —Preschool will move to Spring Ahead Learning Center," Lime Springs Herald, January 16, 2015, https://limespringsherald.wordpress.com/2015/01/16/lime-springs-school-to-close-preschool-will-move-to-spring-ahead-learning-center/#more-4513

35   "Lime Springs Herald publishes last newspaper after 139 years," KWWL, February 11, 2015, http://www.kwwl.com/story/28087438/2015/02/Wednesday/lime-springs-herald-publishes-last-newspaper-after-139-years

36   Wolfgang Saxon, "Frank P. Briggs, 98, a Publisher And Truman's Senate Successor," The New York Times, September 25, 1992, https://www.nytimes.com/1992/09/25/us/frank-p-briggs-98-a-publisher-and-truman-s-senate-successor.html

37   Alicia Stice, "Macon County left with one newspaper after shuttering of Chronicle-Herald," Columbia Daily Tribune, August 30, 2014, http://www.columbiatribune.com/201c66a4-45d0-56e5-8d4b-6472b64ea840.html

38   1996 Pulitzer Prizes, https://www.pulitzer.org/prize-winners-by-year/1996

39   Pew Research Center analysis of Bureau of Labor Statistics Occupational Employment Statistics data, June 13, 2018: http://www.journalism.org/fact-sheet/newspapers/

40   Sarah Cavanah, "Measuring Metropolitan Newspaper Pullback and Its Effects on Political Participation," Retrieved from the University of Minnesota Digital Conservancy, 2016, http://hdl.handle.net/11299/182213.
      See also: Lee Shaker, "Dead Newspapers and Citizens' Civic Engagement» Communication Faculty Publications and Presentations, 2014, https://pdxscholar.library.pdx.edu/comm_fac/17

41   Information on distribution of newspapers from Standard Rate and Data Service, Print Media Circulation, 1992

42   Information on distribution of newspapers from Standard Rate and Data Service, Print Media Circulation, 2018

43   2001 Pulitzer Prizes https://www.pulitzer.org/prize-winners-by-year/2001

44   Information on distribution of newspapers from Standard Rate and Data Service, Print Media Circulation, 2004 and 2018

45   Nick Madigan, "An Abrupt End to the Tampa Tribune After a Blow Delivered by Its Rival," The New York Times, May 20, 2016, https://www.nytimes.com/2016/05/21/business/media/an-abrupt-end-to-the-tampa-tribune-after-a-blow-from-its-rival.html
      See also: Susan Taylor Martin, Richard Danielson, "Tampa Bay Times Purchases Tampa Tribune," Tampa Bay Times, May 3, 2016, http://www.tampabay.com/news/business/tampa-bay-times-purchases-tampa-tribune/2275765

46   Richard Pérez-Peña, "Rocky Mountain News Is Closing in Denver," The New York Times, February 26, 2009, https://www.nytimes.com/2009/02/27/business/media/27paper.html?mtrref=www.google.com&mtrref=undefined

47   Patrick Oppmann, "Seattle Post-Intelligencer prints final edition in online transition," CNN, March 17, 2009, http://www.cnn.com/2009/US/03/16/pi.closes/index.html

48   Steven Waldman, "The Information Needs of Communities: The changing media landscape in a broadband age," Federal Communications Commission, July 2011, https://transition.fcc.gov/osp/inc-report/The_Information_Needs_of_Communities.pdf

49   Martin Kaplan and Matthew Hale, "Local TV News in the Los Angeles Media Market: Are Stations Serving the Public Interest?" The Norman Lear Center, University of Southern California Annenberg School for Communication & Journalism, March 11, 2010, https://learcenter.org/pdf/LANews2010.pdf.

50   Pengjie Gao, Chang Lee, Dermot Murphy, Financing Dies in Darkness? The Impact of Newspaper Closures on Public Finance (August 10, 2018). Available at SSRN: https://ssrn.com/abstract=3175555 or http://dx.doi.org/10.2139/ssrn.3175555

51   David Bockino, "Three Days a Week: Has A New Production Cycle Altered The Times-Picayune's News Coverage?" Paper presented at the annual meeting of the Association for Education in Journalism and Mass Communication, Renaissance Hotel, Washington DC, Aug 08, 2013

52   Amy Maestas, "Ann Arbor: Citizenship and the Local Newspaper," 2017, Thwarting the Emergence of News Deserts, University of North Carolina-Chapel Hill. See also: Sarah Cavanah, "Measuring Metropolitan Newspaper Pullback and Its Effects on Political Participation," 2016, Retrieved from the University of Minnesota Digital Conservancy, http://hdl.handle.net/11299/182213.

53   Philip M. Napoli, Matthew Weber, Katie Mccollough, Qun Wang, Assessing Local Journalism: News Deserts, Journalism Divides, and the Determinants of the Robustness of Local News, DeWitt Wallace Center for Media and Democracy, Duke University, August 2018

54   Tom Mast, "Star-Tribune acquires Casper Journal," Casper Star-Tribune, October 30, 2004, https://trib.com/news/local/star-tribune-acquires-casper-journal/article_fe93f894-e8a3-510e-92b8-ad15a6f17dd9.html
      See also: 2017 Research interview with then Wyoming Press Association Executive Director Jim Angell

"The Casper Journal has moved to Trib.com," Casper Journal, February 13, 2017, https://trib.com/casperjournal/the-casper-journal-has-moved-to-trib-com/article_a068d6cf-1a45-5024-a4b2-d6c40e-a1765b.html

"Tired of the Casper Journal Littering Your Lawn? Here's How to Stop Delivery," 95.5 My Country, May 24, 2017, http://mycountry955.com/tired-of-the-casper-journal-littering-your-lawn-heres-how-to-stop-delivery/

55   Research interview with Sara Glines, Publisher, The Raleigh News & Observer, September 4, 2018.
        See also: John Drescher, "Community papers to focus on food, dining," News and Observer, June 2, 2017, https://www.newsobserver.com/news/local/news-columns-blogs/john-drescher/article154090344.html

        "N&O journalists collect 39 NC press awards," News & Observer, February 26, 2016, https://www.newsobserver.com/news/local/article62662457.html

56   "10/13 Communications announces sale of Houston Community News and Media Group to Hearst Newspapers, LLC," Cribb. Greene and Cope, August 10, 2016, http://www.cribb.com/release/2016/08-10-houston-community-news-and-media-group.html

57   Sasha Lekach, "Fewer than half of newspaper jobs from 15 years ago still exist," Mashable, April 4, 2017, https://mashable.com/2017/04/04/newspaper-publishers-jobs-decline-bls/#gcBl3bVyHsqx

58   Bureau of Labor Statistics, Employment Statistics Survey, 2018, https://data.bls.gov/timeseries/CES1021210001

59   American Society of News Editors, 2008 and 2015 Newsroom Diversity Survey Census, 2008, 2015 https://www.asne.org/diversity-survey-2008; https://www.asne.org/diversity-survey-2015.
        See also: Bob Papper, "TV News Employment surpasses newspapers," Radio Television Digital News Association/Hofstra University Newsroom Survey, April 16, 2018 https://rtdna.org/uploads/files/2018%20RTDNA%20Newsroom%20Staffing%20Research.pdf

60   The New York Daily News' Pulitzers," New York Daily News, 2018, http://interactive.nydailynews.com/pulitzers/

61   Andrea Chang," Tronc cuts dozens of employees, including former Times Editor Lewis D'Vorkin," April 12, 2018, http://www.latimes.com/business/la-fi-tronc-layoffs-20180412-story.html
        See also: Liana B. Baker, "Tronc buys New York Daily News in push into No. 1 media market," Reuters, September 4, 2017, https://www.reuters.com/article/us-daily-news-m-a-tronc/tronc-buys-new-york-daily-news-idUSKCN1BG09O

        Benjamin Hart, "The Ax Falls at the Daily News," Daily Intelligencer, July 23, 2018, http://nymag.com/daily/intelligencer/2018/07/behind-the-scenes-as-the-new-york-daily-news-staff-cuts.html

        Keith J. Kelly, "Daily News mass layoffs even worse than first reported," New York Post, July 24, 2018 https://nypost.com/2018/07/24/daily-news-massacre-even-worse-than-first-reported/

        Jaclyn Peiser, "Daily News Newsroom Cut in Half by Tronc as Top Editor Is Ousted," The New York Times, July 23, 2018 https://www.nytimes.com/2018/07/23/business/media/tronc-daily-news-layoffs.html

62   Ian Donnis, "Twenty-two Guild Layoffs At The Providence Journal Include Bob Kerr," Rhode Island Public Radio, September 2, 2014, http://www.ripr.org/post/twenty-two-guild-layoffs-providence-journal-include-bob-kerr#stream/0
        See also: Alan Rosenberg, "The Providence Journal's 188th-birthday mystery," Providence Journal, July 15, 2017, http://www.providencejournal.com/news/20170715/alan-rosenberg-providence-journals-188th-birthday-mystery

        "More staff reductions at Projo and Big Price Increase," GoLocalProv, July 11, 2018, http://m.golocalprov.com/business/more-staff-reductions-at-projo-and-big-price-increase

        Ian Donnis, "Providence Newspaper Guild Protests GateHouse's Management of Projo," Rhode Island Public Radio, May 4, 2016, http://www.ripr.org/post/providence-newspaper-guild-protests-gatehouses-management-projo#stream/0

        Tom Grubisich, "GateHouse Media's Kirk Davis Argues Chain Is Becoming a 'Leader in Community Engagement," Street Fight, May 31, 2018, https://streetfightmag.com/2018/05/31/gatehouse-medias-kirk-davis-argues-chain-is-becoming-a-leader-in-community-engagement/

63   Julie Reynolds, "Working under a hedge fund: how billionaires made the crisis at America's newspapers even worse," dfmworkers.org, April 10, 2017, https://dfmworkers.org/working-under-a-hedge-fund-how-billionaires-made-the-crisis-at-americas-newspapers-even-worse/ Joe Nocera, "Alden Global Capital's Business Model Destroys Newspapers for Little Gain," Bloomberg, March 26, 2018, https://www.bloomberg.com/view/articles/2018-03-26/alden-global-capital-s-business-model-destroys-newspapers-for-little-gain

64   Population from United States Census Bureau: Delaware County, Pennsylvania, 2017 https://www.census.gov/quickfacts/fact/table/delawarecountypennsylvania/PST045217
      Circulation from: Alliance for Audited Media, Q2, 2018

65   Bob Fernandez, "Philly's Digital First papers face harsh cuts, potential 'lights-out scenario'," Philadelphia Inquirer, May 15,2018, http://www2.philly.com/philly/business/digital-first-media-philly-papers-cuts-profits-hedge-fund-dissent-20180515.html
      See also: Julie Reynolds, "Working under a hedge fund: how billionaires made the crisis at America's newspapers even worse," dfmworkers.org, April 10, 2017, https://dfmworkers.org/working-under-a-hedge-fund-how-billionaires-made-the-crisis-at-americas-newspapers-even-worse/

66   Discussion among participants at North Carolina City and County Communicators, 11th Annual Conference, April 19, 2018, New Bern, North Carolina, http://nc3c.com/images/meeting/041818/draft_2018_nc3c_conference_agenda__003_.pdf

67   Pengjie Gao, Chang Lee, Dermot Murphy, Financing Dies in Darkness? The Impact of Newspaper Closures on Public Finance. August 10, 2018, Available at SSRN: https://ssrn.com/abstract=3175555 or http://dx.doi.org/10.2139/ssrn.3175555.

68   Judith Miller, "News Deserts: No News Is Bad News," Urban Policy 2018, Manhattan Institute, October 2, 2018, https://www.manhattan-institute.org/html/urban-policy-2018-news-deserts-no-news-bad-news-11510.html

69   Measured by total number of newspapers owned, instead of total circulation.

70   Transaction stats from Dirks, Van Essen, Murray and April, Year-End 2017, December 31, 2017, http://dirksvanessen.com/articles/view/227/year-end-2017/ and Dirks, Van Essen, Murray and April, Q2 2018, July 1, 2018, http://dirksvanessen.com/articles/view/231/2nd-quarter-2018/

71   Rick Kelley, "AIM Media buys Civitas Media properties in major acquisition," Brownsville Herald, June 13, 2017, https://www.brownsvilleherald.com/news/local/aim-media-buys-civitas-media-properties-in-major-acquisition/article_35d90584-50ab-11e7-99f9-e70746dbf83f.html
      See also: "Boone affiliate acquires Kentucky and Tennessee newspapers," September 11, 2017, http://www.boonenewspapers.com/2017/09/boone-affiliate-acquires-kentucky-and-tennessee-newspapers/

72   "10/13 Communications announces sale of Houston Community News and Media Group to Hearst Newspapers, LLC," Cribb. Greene and Cope, August 10, 2016, http://www.cribb.com/release/2016/08-10-houston-community-news-and-media-group.html
      See also: "Dallas Area Newspaper Cluster Sold to S.A.W. Advisors, LLC," Cribb, Greene and Cope, October 17, 2016, http://www.editorandpublisher.com/news/dallas-area-newspaper-cluster-sold-to-s-a-w-advisors-llc/
      "Independent Newsmedia acquires 4 West Valley newspapers," Scottsdale Independent, June 21, 2016, https://www.scottsdaleindependent.com/news/independent-newsmedia-acquires-4-west-valley-newspapers/

73   "Company Overview," New Media Investment Group, May 3, 2018, http://ir.newmediainv.com/ Presentations

74   "Investing in Newspapers in 2018," Key Executives Mega-Conference Panel Discussion, San Diego, February 27, 2018 http://snpa.static2.adqic.com/static/2018MegaProgram.pdf

75   Gilbert Baez, "Fayetteville Observer sold to GateHouse Media," WRAL, July 28, 2016, https://www.wral.com/fayetteville-observer-sold-to-gatehouse-media/15884799/
      See also: Robert Kuttner, Hildy Zenger, "Saving the Free Press from Private Equity," American Prospect, December 27, 2017, http://prospect.org/article/saving-free-press-private-equity

76   "Thwarting the Emergence of News Deserts", UNC Center for Innovation and Sustainability in Local Media, 2017

77   Dirks, Van Essen, Murray and April, Year-End 2017, December 31, 2017, http://dirksvanessen.com/articles/view/227/year-end-2017/

78   "Hearst Acquires Print, Digital and Local Media Assets of 21st Century Media Newspaper, LLC, Including the New Haven Register," Hearst, June 5, 2017

79   "Hearst Purchases Locally-Focused Houston Community Newspapers & Media Group," Hearst, July 29, 2016, http://www.hearst.com/newsroom/hearst-purchases-locally-focused-houston-community-newspapers-media-group

80   2018 UNC Database, Center for Innovation and Sustainability in Local Media

81   "Akron Beacon Journal sold to GateHouse Media," Crain's Cleveland Business, April 11, 2018, http://www.crainscleveland.com/article/20180411/news/157966/akron-beacon-journal-sold-gatehouse-media

82   David C. Coulson, Stephen Lacy, Daniel Riffe, "Group Ownership Increases among Weekly Newspapers," January 1, 2014, Newspaper Research Journal, Vol 35, Issue 1, pp. 36 - 50

83   Brian Wieser, Pivotal, December 2017, https://www.cnbc.com/2017/12/20/google-facebook-digital-ad-marketshare-growth-pivotal.html

84   "East End weeklies announce joint effort to examine the opioid crisis," The Suffolk Times, December 12, 2017, http://suffolktimes.timesreview.com/2017/12/79428/east-end-weeklies-announce-joint-effort-examine-opioid-crisis/

85   Steven Waldman, "The Information Needs of Communities: The changing media landscape in a broadband age," Federal Communications Commission, July 2011, https://transition.fcc.gov/osp/inc-report/The_Information_ Needs_of_Communities.pdf

86   Bob Papper, "TV News Employment surpasses newspapers," Radio Television Digital News Association/Hofstra University Newsroom Survey, April 16, 2018 https://rtdna.org/uploads/files/2018%20RTDNA%20Newsroom%20Staffing%20Research.pdf

87   Amy Mitchell, Jeffrey Gottfried, Michael Barthel, Elisa Shearer, "The Modern News Consumer," Pew Research Center, Knight Foundation, July 7, 2016, http://www.journalism.org/2016/07/07/pathways-to-news/

88   "Local TV News and the New Media Landscape," Knight Foundation, April 5, 2018 https://knightfoundation.org/reports/local-tv-news-and-the-new-media-landscape

89   American Society of News Editors, 2008 Newsroom Diversity Survey Census, 2008, https://www.asne.org/diversity-survey-2008; https://www.asne.org/diversity-survey-2015

90   Katerina Eva Matsa, "Fewer Americans rely on TV news; what type they watch varies by who they are," January 5, 2018, http://www.pewresearch.org/fact-tank/2018/01/05/fewer-americans-rely-on-tv-news-what-type-they-watch-varies-by-who-they-are/

91   "Local TV News and the New Media Landscape," Knight Foundation, April 5, 2018 https://knightfoundation.org/reports/local-tv-news-and-the-new-media-landscape

92   Justin Blankenship, "What Makes the News? TV's Coverage of Rural Communities," Thwarting the Emergence of News Deserts, 2017, http://newspaperownership.com/wp-content/uploads/2017/03/Symposium-Leave-Behind-Web-Final.pdf
      See also: Steven Waldman, "The Information Needs of Communities: The changing media landscape in a broadband age," Federal Communications Commission, July 2011, https://transition.fcc.gov/osp/inc-report/The_Information_ Needs_of_Communities.pdf
      Martin Kaplan and Matthew Hale, "Local TV News in the Los Angeles Media Market: Are Stations Serving the Public Interest?" The Norman Lear Center, University of Southern California Annenberg School for Communication & Journalism, March 11, 2010, https://learcenter.org/pdf/LANews2010.pdf

93   "Local TV News and the New Media Landscape," Knight Foundation, April 5, 2018 https://knightfoundation.org/reports/local-tv-news-and-the-new-media-landscape

94   "Local TV News and the New Media Landscape," Knight Foundation, April 5, 2018 https://knightfoundation.org/reports/local-tv-news-and-the-new-media-landscape

95   "Local TV News and the New Media Landscape," Knight Foundation, April 5, 2018 https://knightfoundation.org/reports/local-tv-news-and-the-new-media-landscape

96   "Local TV News and the New Media Landscape," Knight Foundation, April 5, 2018 https://knightfoundation.org/reports/local-tv-news-and-the-new-media-landscape

97   H.R.4103 - Cable Franchise Policy and Communications Act of 1984, 1984, https://www.congress.gov/bill/98th-congress/house-bill/4103

98   According to estimates from American Community Television (ACT) http://acommunitytv.org/

99   Research Interview with Alliance for Community Media CEO Mike Wassenaar, August 3, 2018

100   Membership List, Alliance for Community Media, 2018, http://www.allcommunitymedia.org/membershiplist

101   Research Interview at Alliance for Community Media Annual Conference, Baltimore, Maryland, July 12, 2018

102   Research Interview at Alliance for Community Media Annual Conference, Baltimore, Maryland, July 12, 2018

103   Based on a randomized spot analysis of 28 online news sites from a database of more than 500 to determine type of news content distributed.

104   Local TV News and the New Media Landscape," Knight Foundation, April 5, 2018 https://knightfoundation.org/reports/local-tv-news-and-the-new-media-landscape

105   Howard Owens, "Tom Rivers makes the leap from print to online news with new site serving Orleans County," The Batavian, April 2, 2013 https://www.thebatavian.com/howard-owens/tom-rivers-makes-leap-print-online-news-new-site-serving-orleans-county/36777
      See also: "About Orleans Hub," Orleans Hub, 2018, https://orleanshub.com/about-orleanshub-com/

106   "About the Center," Kentucky Center for Public Service Journalism, https://www.kycpsj.com/about-the-center/

107   "Gaining Ground: How Nonprofit News Ventures Seek Sustainability," Knight Foundation, April 2015, https://www.knightfoundation.org/features/nonprofitnews-2015/

108   Matthew Nisbet et al.,"Funding the News: Foundations and Nonprofit Media," Shorenstein Center on Media, Politics and Public Policy at the Harvard Kennedy School and Northeastern University's School of Journalism, June 18, 2018 https://shorensteincenter.org/funding-the-news-foundations-and-non profit-media/

109   Tim Griggs, "VTDigger: A Rising Star in Nonprofit News," Institute for Nonprofit News, May 21, 2018, https://inn.org/2018/05/vtdigger-a-rising-star-in-nonprofit-news/

110   VTDigger, 2016 Annual Report, https://ja3ga476chj1nc6csy2j81c7-wpengine.netdna-ssl.com/wp-content/uploads/2017/10/VTD_2016_AnnualReport-FINAL-FT.pdf

111   Grantors," VTDigger, 2018, https://vtdigger.org/about-vtdigger/grantors/
      See also: About the Community Foundation," The Vermont Community Foundation, 2018, https://www.vermontcf.org/AboutUs/AbouttheCommunityFoundation.aspx

112   "Media Kit," VTDigger, 2018, https://vtdigger.org/media-kit/

113   United States Census Bureau: Flint city, Michigan, 2017, https://www.census.gov/quickfacts/fact/table/flintcitymichigan/INC110216

114   About Us," Flint Beat, 2018, http://flintbeat.com/about-us-2/

115   GoFundMe: Flint Beat, 2017, https://www.gofundme.com/flintbeat

116   Kristen Hare, "She knew how to cover Flint. Now she's figuring out how to make that coverage sustainable," Poynter, September 5, 2018, https://www.poynter.org/news/she-knew-how-cover-flint-now-shes-figuring-out-how-make-coverage-sustainable

117   United States Census Bureau: Percent of Households with a Broadband Internet Subscription, 2017 American Community Survey: https://factfinder.census.gov/faces/tableservices/jsf/pages/product view.xhtml?pid=ACS_16_1YR_GCT2801.US05PR&prodType=table

118   Research Interview with LION Executive Director Matt DeRienzo, June 11, 2018

119   Kristen Hare, "She knew how to cover Flint. Now she's figuring out how to make that coverage sustainable," Poynter, September 5, 2018, https://www.poynter.org/news/she-knew-how-cover-flint-now-shes-figuring-out-how-make-coverage-sustainable

120   Local TV News and the New Media Landscape," Knight Foundation, April 5, 2018 https://knightfoundation.org/reports/local-tv-news-and-the-new-media-landscape

121   Penelope Muse Abernathy, Saving Community Journalism: The Path to Profitability, (Chapel Hill: UNC Press, 2014)

122   Penelope Muse Abernathy, Joann Sciarrino, The Strategic Digital Media Entrepreneur, (Wiley Blackwell: 2018)

123   James T. Hamilton, All the News That's Fit to Sell: How the Market Transforms Information into News, Princeton University Press, 2004, JSTOR, www.jstor.org/stable/j.ctt7smgs.

124   Christopher Ali, "The Merits of Merit Goods: Local Journalism and Public Policy in a Time of Austerity." Journal of Information Policy 6, 2016

125   Matthew Nisbet et al."Funding the News: Foundations and Nonprofit Media," Shorenstein Center on Media, Politics and Public Policy at the Harvard Kennedy School and Northeastern University's School of Journalism, June 18, 2018 https://shorensteincenter.org/funding-the-news-foundations-and-nonprofit-media/

126   Brian Wieser, Pivotal, December 2017, https://www.cnbc.com/2017/12/20/google-facebook-digital-ad-marketshare-growth-pivotal.html

127   Judith Miller, "News Deserts: No News Is Bad News," Urban Policy 2018, Manhattan Institute, October 2, 2018, https://www.manhattan-institute.org/html/urban-policy-2018-news-deserts-no-news-bad-news-11510.html;
       See also: Lina M. Khan, Amazon's Antitrust Paradox, 126 Yale L.J. (2016). Available at: http://digital-commons.law.yale.edu/ylj/vol126/iss3/3

128   Alphabet Inc., Facebook, SEC 10-K Filings, 2018

129   Michael Cormack, Jr., Knight Commission on Trust, Media and Democracy, April 29, 2018, Nashville, Tennessee https://www.aspeninstitute.org/programs/communications-and-society-program/recap-nashville-forum/

130   Research Interview with LION Executive Director Matt DeRienzo, June 11, 2018

131   Penelope Abernathy, Knight Commission on Trust, Media and Democracy, April 29, 2018, Nashville, Tennessee https://www.cislm.org/how-to-restore-trust-in-the-media-abernathys-testimony-to-the-knight-commission/

THE ENDURING LEGACY OF THE NEW MEDIA BARONS

How Private Equity and Hedge Funds Changed Newspapers

Less than a decade ago, in the wake of the worst recession since World War II, a group of private equity and hedge fund investors swooped in to purchase hundreds of financially struggling newspapers, many in bankruptcy. The managers of these funds promised shareholders they had the golden touch and would be able to quickly turn around the fortunes of mature enterprises through a combination of cost cutting and innovative business practices. But the turnaround has proved to be harder than expected, and 2018 may well be a pivotal year for the newspaper industry as these newly minted media barons decide whether to head for the exit or increase their stake.

At the beginning of the year, five of the 10 largest newspaper chains were owned by hedge funds, private equity firms and other types of investment groups, which have vast portfolios of unrelated holdings such as real estate, financial services, international debt and health care companies. By the end of 2018, there may be only two of these companies still actively investing in newspapers: New Media/GateHouse, the largest newspaper company in the country with 451 papers, and Digital First, the third largest with 158 papers. Faced with disappointing returns, the other three large investment-owned chains – Community Newspaper Holdings Inc. (CNHI), tronc/Tribune Publishing and BH Media, which together own almost 300 papers – are either exploring sales of their newspapers or opting out of day-to-day management.

Yet, despite their shrinking number and their relatively short tenure as media moguls, the large investment firms have left an indelible mark on the country's news landscape, which has experienced unprecedented structural change and technological disruption over the past decade.

The investment firms introduced a new way of thinking about the business management of newspapers and their journalistic mission, which often ran counter to the historic practices of traditional print newspaper companies. The standard operating formula often included aggressive cost-cutting, the adoption of advertiser-friendly policies, the sale or shuttering of under-performing newspapers, and financial restructuring, including bankruptcy. At the most extreme, their strategies have led to the closure of hundreds of local papers and diminished the important civic role of newspapers in providing reliable news and information that helps residents of a community make important decisions about governance and quality of life issues.

WHERE THE LARGEST INVESTMENT COMPANIES OWN NEWSPAPERS: 2018

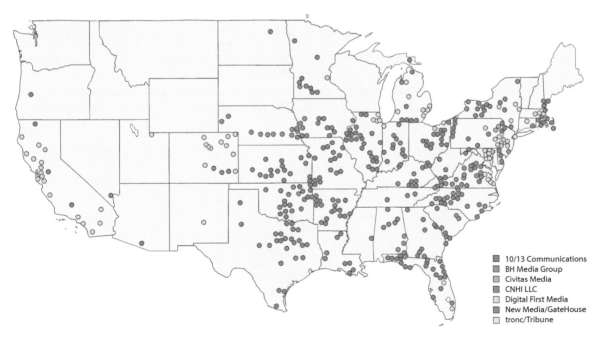

Seven investment groups own 882 newspapers in 41 states.
Source: UNC Database

As the traditional business model for print newspapers has collapsed, many of the business practices introduced by the investment firms have been incorporated into the strategies pursued by legacy newspaper companies, both the large publicly traded chains, as well as the private ones. This raises a number of questions about the future of local newspapers, which have historically been the prime source of news and information in communities throughout the country. What will become of the thousands of newspapers now being sold to the highest bidder? What about the future of the hundreds of papers that remain under the management of hedge funds and private equity companies? Is this retreat by the large investment groups an admission of defeat that will prompt new strategies?

Here are the strategies and tactics introduced by the investment firms that have the most potential to continue altering the local news landscape in the near future:

A willingness to sell or close underperforming papers.

Prior to 2008, large chains typically paid 13 times annual earnings for a newspaper. This meant purchasers needed to own a paper for at least 13 years in order to recoup their investment, so they would typically "buy and hold" a paper for years. In the wake of the Great Recession of 2008, the price of newspapers dropped dramatically. Even the most iconic dailies could be acquired for three to five times annual earnings. At these depressed prices, purchasers could potentially sell or "flip" a newspaper in five years or less and make a profit. Over the past decade and a half, almost half of all newspapers in the country have changed ownership; many have been sold two or more times. If investment firms cannot sell underperforming newspapers, they close them, leaving hundreds of communities without local news outlets. Since 2004, more than 1,800 newspapers, mostly weeklies, have been closed or merged with other papers. For example, Versa Capital Management formed Civitas Media in 2012 when it combined four small newspaper chains that it had purchased in bankruptcy proceedings the previous year. In 2013, Civitas closed eight suburban weeklies in North Carolina and Ohio because "the suburban newspaper isn't a fit in (our) business model," according to Civitas CEO Michael Bush.[1] In 2016 and 2017, Civitas effectively exited the market by selling all but four of the remaining 90 newspapers in its chain to nine different companies.

Reliance on aggressive cost cutting that leads to diminished investment in news operations.

"The thing that we always have to think about and remember is that our first objective is always what's the best thing for our shareholders," said Mike Reed in a June 2018 interview. Reed is CEO of the New Media Investment Group, which owns and operates the Gatehouse chain of newspapers.[2] This emphasis on shareholder return has led to aggressive cost-cutting in many newsrooms, as print revenues and profits continue to decline. Widespread cuts affect all aspects of local news coverage, from routine government meetings to the arts. While overall newsroom staffing declined by nearly a quarter between 2012 and 2017[3], Digital First Media cut staffing by more than half during the same period, in an effort to boost profit despite declining revenues.[4] At the Denver Post alone, Digital First has reduced newsroom staffing by nearly two-thirds over the past five years.[5] The Digital First chain had a profit margin of 17 percent in 2017, one of the highest in the industry.[6] This year, both Gatehouse and Digital First experienced pushback on their newsroom strategies from community activists and concerned residents, as well as journalists who sought to unionize.

Outsourcing of news and sales operations to remote locations, and the establishment of regional publishers and editors, responsible for several newspapers.

Both practices tend to weaken the ties of a local newspaper to its community. While this streamlines the cost of producing a newspaper, the editors in remote locations often lack knowledge of local hot-button issues, and the sales staff and group publishers are often unfamiliar with the specific needs of small businesses in various communities. Editing, design and marketing operations for more than 200 papers owned by GateHouse throughout the U.S. are handled in a center in Austin, Texas.[7] GateHouse has also pioneered the concept of appointing publishers and editors at a larger newspaper to be responsible for the day-to-day supervision and decision-making for other smaller papers in the same geographic region, permanently eliminating those high-paying positions at the smaller publications.[8] This trend in consolidation and outsourcing leads to the merger of papers, resulting in further cutbacks in newsroom staffing. This, in turn, leads to a lack of coverage of local issues that may affect residents of one town, but not others. Digital First has been among the most aggressive merging and consolidating papers, including the eight papers it acquired in the San Francisco Bay area from Media News in 2010 that have been merged into only two papers.[9]

NEWSPAPERS AQUIRED, SOLD, MERGED OR CLOSED
BY THE 7 LARGEST INVESTMENT OWNERS: 2004-2018

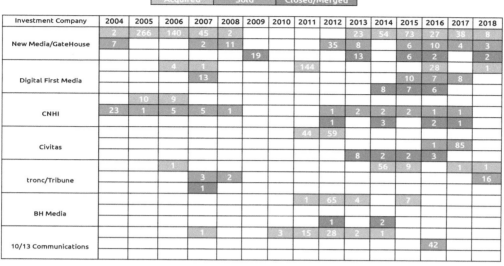

Legend: Acquired | Sold | Closed/Merged

Investment Company	2004	2005	2006	2007	2008	2009	2010	2011	2012	2013	2014	2015	2016	2017	2018
New Media/GateHouse (acquired)	2	266	140	45	2					23	54	73	27	38	8
New Media/GateHouse (sold)	7			2	11				35	8		6	10	4	3
New Media/GateHouse (closed/merged)						19				13		6	2		2
Digital First Media (acquired)			4	1				144					28		1
Digital First Media (sold)				13								10	7	8	
Digital First Media (closed/merged)											8	7	6		
CNHI (acquired)		10	9												
CNHI (sold)	23	1	5	5	1				1	2	2	2	1	1	
CNHI (closed/merged)									1		3		2	1	
Civitas (acquired)								44	59						
Civitas (sold)													1	85	
Civitas (closed/merged)										8	2	2	3		
tronc/Tribune (acquired)			1								56	9		1	1
tronc/Tribune (sold)				3	2										16
tronc/Tribune (closed/merged)				1											
BH Media (acquired)								1	65	4		7			
BH Media (sold)										1		2			
10/13 Communications (acquired)				1			3	15	28	2	1				
10/13 Communications (sold)													42		

Note: The newspaper reflected here may not necessarily match totals shown in press releases, which may include non-community newspapers (i.e. shoppers, business journals, etc.)

Source: UNC Database and Various Press Releases

An aggressive push to grow bigger and bigger.

Consolidation typically occurs in mature industries with declining revenue and profitability. In the short-term, by acquiring other newspapers, newspaper companies can show year-over-year revenue growth, while simultaneously shoring up the bottom line by consolidating and cutting costs across several papers. Long-term, there is a prevailing strategic assumption that, in order to attract both print and digital advertising revenue, local newspapers need to have a large geographic and circulation footprint that extends across several markets. Therefore, in recent years, the largest chains have shifted their focus away from small markets, which was the initial focus of the large investment firms, toward papers in mid-sized and large markets, such as Austin, Texas, or Boston. GateHouse has been the most aggressive newspaper acquirer in the country, spending more than $1 billion[10] on 200 newspaper acquisitions since 2013.

Aggressive adoption of advertiser- and business-friendly policies and practices.

In some cases, investment firms have prioritized advertiser needs over those of the consumers of its news, leading to cutbacks in the newsroom funding. Randy Miller, founder and president of 10/13 Communications, a chain of 45 papers, repeatedly emphasized throughout the company's nearly 10-year existence that newsroom staffing should be kept at a minimum and sales staffing should be kept at a maximum.[11] The sales practices introduced by the investment firms – and adopted by other large chains – are pushing up against well-established norms and traditions that have separated editorial coverage from advertiser concerns. Newspapers are forced to rethink and often redefine the "wall" between editorial and advertising content. Many companies have set up in-house digital agencies that offer everything from corporate videos to social media communication strategies. The GateHouse chain, which is owned by the Fortress Investment Group, is pushing the envelope further, and raising questions about the role of a local newspaper's sales department in supporting local businesses. GateHouse is offering newspaper advertisers everything from small business loans (arranged through a subsidiary of the Fortress Investment Group) to IT support (also offered through a Fortress subsidiary). When a GateHouse representative approaches an advertiser, is that person acting as the sales representative of a local newspaper, or as a loan officer and technology expert with one of Fortress' other subsidiaries?

Despite the pursuit of these strategies and practices, the seven largest investment companies have produced mixed to poor results for their shareholders, and often lagged behind the performance and benchmarks of other companies. With names like Digital First and "tronc" (short for Tribune Online

Content), one might also expect these companies to be at the forefront of digital innovation. However, the major investment owners have proven slow to adapt to a viable digital model that offsets print revenue declines. In fact, they have often been outpaced in their transformation by traditional newspaper chains.

The large investment-owned newspapers chains are often part of a larger portfolios of assets held by public or private equity-based firms or hedge and pension funds. The New Media/Gatehouse newspapers, for example, are a subsidiary of Fortress, which is owned by Japanese telecommunications conglomerate, the Softbank Group. Digital First is owned by Alden Capital, which manages a portfolio that includes a Canadian pharmacy chain and foreign debt holdings. BH Media is part of the Berkshire Hathaway equity group, and CNHI is a subsidiary of the Retirement Systems of Alabama portfolio.

The investment firms actively manage their vast portfolios of properties. Newspaper revenues and profits often account for a very small fraction of the revenues generated by the vast portfolios worth billions of dollars held by the investment entities. Therefore, if newspaper chains perform, they are retained in the portfolio of assets. If they fail to meet expectations, they are either sold, or management is passed off to another company.

At a time when many newspapers are struggling to maintain single digit profit margins, both New Media/ GateHouse and Digital First are vying with one another to buy more papers, whereupon they immediately introduce a round of cost cutting in an attempt to extract double- digit returns. In a quarterly call with analysts in May, Softbank executives indicated that they were pleased with the returns Fortress had achieved with the GateHouse chain. Similarly, despite calls from journalists and community activists to sell the Digital First papers, Alden Capital has given no indication that it is ready to exit the newspaper business since Digital First is producing double-digit profit margins that offset losses in other divisions.

In contrast, the Retirement Systems of Alabama, which established CNHI in 1998, decided in June to put the chain of 114 papers up for sale. Also in June, Warren Buffett, frustrated at the lackluster returns on his chain of 75 newspapers, turned over day-to-day management of BH Media to Lee Enterprises, a publicly traded chain with 100 papers. Tronc/Tribune, which has 77 papers and been has been repeatedly frustrated in its attempts to buy or merge with other papers or chains, is seeking new investors and considering a sale of its assets to both private equity companies, as well as publicly traded chains, such as the McClatchy Company. Two other chains, Civitas and 10/13 Communications, sold almost all of their 145 papers in 2016 and 2017.

At the beginning of 2018, the large investment groups owned almost 900 papers in 42 states. Here's how these media barons are positioned in the final months of 2018:

TOP 7 INVESTMENT FIRMS RANKED BY NUMBER OF PAPERS OWNED: 2018

Rank	Company	Total Papers	Daily Papers	Total Circ. (000s)	Daily Circ. (000s)
1	New Media/GateHouse	451	153	4,445	2,805
2	Digital First Media	158	51	3,241	2,016
3	CNHI	114	73	1,006	707
4	tronc/Tribune	77	17	2,462	1,705
5	BH Media Group	75	33	1,216	908
6	Civitas Media	4	1	36	24
7	10/13 Communications	3	0	83	0
	TOTALS	882	328	12,500	8,164

SOURCE: UNC Database

NEW MEDIA / GATEHOUSE

WHERE NEW MEDIA/GATEHOUSE OWNS NEWSPAPERS: 2018

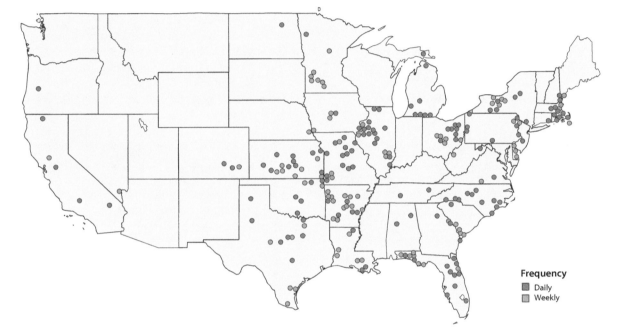

Frequency
- ■ Daily
- ■ Weekly

New Media/GateHouse owns 451 newspapers in 34 states.
Source: UNC Database

New Media/GateHouse: 451 papers in 2018

Publisher Jane Rawlings' remarks to reporters and editors at the 150-year-old Pueblo Chieftain in May 2018 were intended to be reassuring. "I think you will be comforted in what they have to say," she said, referring to GateHouse Media, the new owners of Colorado's oldest continuously published newspaper.[12] Yet, immediately after the announcement of the sale, Rawlings stepped down as publisher of the 33,000 circulation[13] daily and assumed leadership of her family's nonprofit community organization. Within a month, GateHouse executives had announced layoffs of the digital editor and two page designers. The

staff braced for more changes as the new owner announced a hiring freeze and indicated the company would continue to reassess staffing.[14]

The announcement that a newspaper is being sold to GateHouse – the largest newspaper chain in the country — has become commonplace in recent years. Since 2013, the company has spent more than $1 billion on acquisitions, snapping up dozens of papers in 15 states at greatly reduced valuations.[15] Once the company assumes ownership of a newspaper such as the Pueblo Chieftain, it tends to pursue the same cost reduction strategy. It consolidates functions such as copy editing and page design in a remote location. Additionally, specialty and veteran reporters are laid off or severed, and then replaced by general assignment reporters whose journalistic responsibility is to produce "shareable" stories that attract online readers. As a result, GateHouse-owned newsrooms are often half the size within a matter of months.[16] The experience at the Columbia (Missouri) Daily-Tribune, an independently owned paper that Gatehouse purchased in 2016, is typical. Multiple rounds of layoffs have wiped out more than half the newsroom staff of 20, leaving only one full-time state and politics reporter as of February 2018, responsible for covering a community of 120,000 residents. In addition, GateHouse eliminated local columnists and the longtime editorial cartoonist.[17]

The current GateHouse chain, headquartered in New York, was built through an acquisition spree that began in the years after the 2008 recession. In 2014, GateHouse owned 379 newspapers and controlled 3.1 million in circulation. By 2018, the company owned 451 papers and controlled more than 4.3 million in circulation. In its most recent annual financial statement, Gatehouse said it operates in 565 markets in 38 states,[18] a total that includes more than 120 local websites, advertising supplements and business publications. In the last 18 months, GateHouse has completed or announced 11 separate transactions totaling $290 million, often for entire chains. The company has bought more than 25 daily newspapers since 2016.[19]

GateHouse is a division of the Fortress Investment Group, which has a diversified portfolio of investments, ranging from financial services to golf courses and private railroads. Revenue from the newspaper chain represents less than two percent of the $70 billion in revenue generated by the Fortress portfolio. GateHouse aggressively manages its portfolio of papers, selling, closing and merging under-performing papers. Since 2004, GateHouse has sold more than four dozen papers, nearly half of those since 2013. It has also closed five dailies, all with less than 10,000 circulation, in three states – Kansas, Illinois and Missouri. In addition, it has closed or merged dozens of weeklies. Just months after announcing its acquisition of the Austin American Statesman in March 2018, for example, GateHouse said it would close the affiliated Spanish language weekly by October 2018 and offered voluntary severance packages to all of the Statesman's more than 200 employees.[20]

The GateHouse acquisition spree has been fueled by debt. When GateHouse filed for bankruptcy restructuring in 2013 and reemerged under the name of the public holding company New Media Investment Group, the company listed $1.2 billion in debt.[21] In 2017, its total debt equaled $609 million, roughly 14 times its cash flow.[22] New Media Investment Group CEO Mike Reed sees no issue in continuing the scaling and consolidation strategy, as long as newspaper prices remain as they are today, in the three to five times trailing earnings. With Fortress as its parent company, GateHouse has access to capital that allows it to continue buying. "(Fortress) allows us to access capital at better rates at better structures than anybody else is able to in our industry," Reed said in a June 2018 interview with Nieman Lab.[23] "In the structure of our credit agreement…for every dollar that we make, a piece goes to the lenders, but we have full discretion to redeploy that dollar. So we can invest in the business, we can do acquisitions, we can pay dividends to shareholders." In a May 2018 conference call with security analysts, executives at the Japanese telecommunications giant Softbank, which owns Fortress Investment Group, indicated they would support continued expansion of the GateHouse chain, including the major acquisition of another newspaper chain, such as tronc/Tribune, which is seeking investors and entertaining bids.[24]

Often, GateHouse targets independent owners who find it increasingly hard to navigate the financial landmines dotting the local news landscape. The company has paid sellers an average of 4.1 times earnings and targets a range of between 3.5 to 4.5 times earnings.[25] "Scale matters, and the more that we have, the better the opportunity becomes for us to execute on our operational strategy," Reed said. "…I think it's really hard to do things in onesies and twosies. Our hope is to continue to consolidate the industry, with the focus on the types of deals we've been doing in the past, but we can't do them at all costs."[26]

GateHouse has traditionally sought papers in small and mid-sized communities with little media competition. Historically, roughly 40 percent of GateHouse's newspapers have been in rural or low-income communities, with limited media competitions such as regional broadcasting outlets or other news publications. In 2014, the average circulation of its 359 papers – two thirds of which were weeklies –was less than 9,000.[27] Since 2016, it has shifted its strategy and begun targeting daily

NEW MEDIA/GATEHOUSE 2017 FINANCIAL RESULTS

Revenue (2017)	$1.34 bil	Operating Expenses	$1.31 bil
Digital Revenue	$143 mil	Operating Income	$34.6 mil
Percent of Revenue From Digital	11%	Operating Margin	3%

SOURCE: 2017 New Media Investment Group SEC 10-K annual report filing

papers in larger, metro areas such as Providence, Rhode Island; Columbus, Ohio; Austin, Texas, and Palm Beach, Florida. The Austin American Statesman and Palm Beach Post, which GateHouse acquired in 2018, have a circulation of more than 86,000 and 77,500, respectively.[28] GateHouse papers are primarily located in states east of the Rockies – in the central and upper Midwest, South, Mid-Atlantic and New England regions of the country.

However, even as GateHouse continues to boost its revenues year-over-year with acquisitions, the company is experiencing rising costs, dwindling operating margins and declining performance at existing papers. Year-over-year revenues at existing papers fell by nearly 6 percent to $1.3B between 2016 and 2017 while operating income fell by 44 percent to $34.6M. In 2017, GateHouse posted an operating margin of 2.6 percent, down from 8.6 percent in 2015 and 4.8 percent in 2016. While competing newspaper chains have turned to digital to offset traditional revenue declines, GateHouse has been slower to adapt. Digital revenue totaled $143.4 million in 2017, or only slightly more than 10 percent.[29] At Gannett, the second largest newspaper chain in the country behind GateHouse, 2017 digital revenues totaled $994.9M, or a third of total revenue.[30]

GateHouse has sought to combat decreasing operating margins by pivoting to a business-friendly revenue model, offering local businesses everything from mobile app development to small business loans, arranged through one of the financial services companies owned by parent company Fortress. Since 2014, the company has invested $65 million in its business services and financing division, UpCurve, and a marketing division, ThriveHive.[31] UpCurve's revenue has grown from $6 million in 2013 to $71 million in 2017. "We expect (print) declines to continue," Reed said in the company's

2017 earnings call. "However, the point here is, we continue to be less exposed to the print category and more exposed to the relevant and stable and growing revenue categories that we've created."[32]

In contrast, there has been little investment in GateHouse newsrooms.[33] Wages have been stagnant, and employees face the continual threat of further layoffs as print revenue declines. Reed acknowledges that GateHouse lays off "highly paid but unproductive reporters" while asking remaining reporters to write more stories.[34] This had led to union drives at several GateHouse papers in Florida, including the Lakeland Ledger and Sarasota Herald-Tribune in 2016 and the Times-Union in Jacksonville in 2018. A mission statement drafted by the union organizing committee of the 45,000-circulation Times-Union said the 2017 purchase by GateHouse has "brought more uncertainty than perhaps any other time in the newspaper's 154-year history."[35] At the end of 2017, 11 percent of GateHouse's 10,500 employees,[36] were represented by unions. This included employees at such recent purchases as the Providence Journal in Rhode Island and the Erie Times News in Pennsylvania[37]. In September 2017, the NewsGuild-CWA negotiated a one percent pay raise for GateHouse employees it represents.[38]

As robust coverage of routine government meetings and investigative journalism decline at GateHouse-owned papers, readers are also taking notice. Average daily circulation at existing GateHouse papers fell 15 percent between 2014 and 2018, dropping from nearly 16,000 to under 14,000.[39] Circulation at the Daily-Tribune in Columbia, Missouri, has fallen by more than 20 percent to 13,000 in the two years since Gatehouse purchased the paper and eliminated more than half the newsroom staff.[40] In a column in the Daily-Tribune, the GateHouse-installed managing editor, West Virginia native Charles Westmoreland, acknowledged the impact that multiple rounds of layoffs had on the paper's coverage of local issues. "We're still capable of producing impactful journalism, even if there's a little bit less of it at times." he said. "I'd love nothing more than to start adding back to the paper, but that will never happen if readers abandon us during this transition." [41] He pleaded with readers to "please detach yourself from the Tribune of the past and get acquainted with what we are now."

With print advertising and circulation continuing to decline at GateHouse-owned papers, and digital revenue lagging that of competitors such as McClatchy and Gannett, shareholders are also are beginning to take notice. Stock in New Media/ GateHouse sold for as much $25 a share in March 2015. In August 2018, it sold for $16. All of this calls into question how sustainable New Media/ GateHouse's aggressive acquisition and regional roll-up strategy will be long-term, especially as the company pivots away from smaller markets with less competition and focuses, instead, on acquiring dailies in larger, metro areas with numerous media competitors.

DIGITAL FIRST MEDIA

WHERE DIGITAL FIRST MEDIA OWNS NEWSPAPERS: 2018

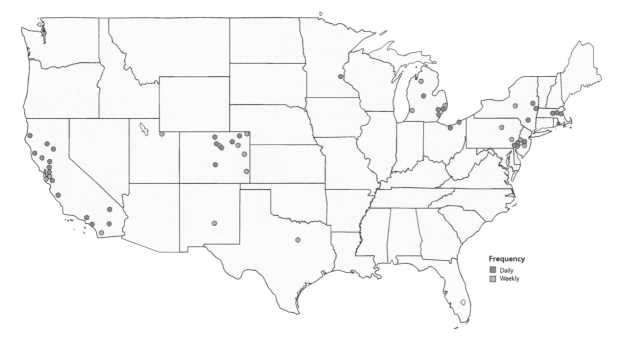

Digital First Media owns 158 newspapers in 12 states.
Source: UNC Database

Digital First Media: 158 papers in 2018

The ruckus started when one hedge fund accused another hedge fund of mismanagement. In March 2018, Solus Alternative Asset Management, which had a minority share in another hedge fund, Alden Global Capital, filed a lawsuit in Delaware, accusing the very secretive Alden fund of siphoning profits from its Digital First newspaper chain to prop up its failed investments in Greek debt and a Canadian pharmacy chain.[42]

As word of the lawsuit leaked, journalists managed to obtain a copy of the 2017 financial results for Digital First and publish it.[43] At a time when other major newspaper chains were struggling to maintain single-digit operating margins, executives at Digital First had posted an operating margin of 17 percent, apparently by cutting newsroom staffing by as much as twice the industry average. In response, journalists at Digital First papers revolted by publishing stories and editorials that criticized Alden for its management of Digital First. With advance notice that yet another round of layoffs was imminent, news executives at the 190,000-circulation[44] Denver Post decided to print a rare front-page editorial on April 8 with the headline, "News Matters: Colo. should demand the newspaper it deserves." The following day Digital First laid off one-third of the Post's remaining newsroom staff of 100. This left the Denver Post, which had 184 journalists in 2012 when it produced the articles that won a Pulitzer Prize for coverage of the Aurora theater shooting, with only 66 journalists covering a metro area of more than 2 million people.[45]

The Denver revolt, which quickly spread to other Digital First newspapers across the country, was covered by news outlets around the world, including The New York Times and Asahi Shimbun in Japan. In May, Digital First employees protested outside the New York office of Alden and attempted to deliver a petition, with 11,000 signatures, demanding that Alden either invest in its Digital First papers or sell them to someone who would. Alden and Digital First management responded by holding firm. The company fired one journalist and threatened to fire others who wrote critical articles.[46] A handful of journalists left in protest. However, Digital First left the mass layoffs in place and quietly filled the vacancies left by the protestors with out-of-state journalists or those hired from digital news sites.

"For a few weeks in the spring and early summer, national attention focused on Denver, Boulder, the Digital First Media chain, and then more broadly on the effects of late capitalism on local American newspapers writ large," wrote Corey Hutchins, a reporter for the Columbia Journalism Review, who also produces a monthly newsletter. "August came with a calm. Things got quiet. A revolution was not realized."[47]

Digital First was formed seven years ago as a subsidiary of Alden Capital when the hedge fund plucked two of the largest newspaper chains in the country out of bankruptcy. Those two chains, MediaNews Group and Journal Register Co., formally merged in 2013 under the Digital First banner. The company name was intended to signify a corporate commitment to transitioning from print to digital. "Project Thunderdome," launched in 2012, provided national and international articles to Digital First newsrooms throughout the country through a centralized hub. But when digital revenues failed to materialize, Digital First abandoned the project in 2014, laying off more than 50 journalists.[48] Shortly after, Alden announced that Digital First was for sale. Although the private equity firm Apollo Global Management expressed interest in purchasing it, Digital First couldn't persuade Apollo to meet its price. Then-CEO John Paton said Alden had concluded the Digital First chain would

not be sold to a single buyer. "There'll be a horse-trading of assets," Paton said in a 2015 interview, adding that the industry should expect Digital First to be both a buyer and seller going forward.[49] In 2014, Digital First owned 208 newspapers and controlled nearly 4.6 million in circulation. Through a combination of merging and selling, the company now owns 158 papers and controls nearly 3.2 million in circulation. In 2016, the company purchased the Orange County Register and Riverside Press-Enterprise in bankruptcy proceedings from Freedom Communications.[50] Both papers have gone through multiple rounds of layoffs and employee buyouts.[51] In March 2018, Digital First outbid GateHouse Media for control of the bankrupt 85,000-circulation[52] Boston Herald. Of the 240 people employed by the paper in December 2017, only 175 reportedly received job offers from Digital First.[53]

Simultaneously, Digital First has been shedding papers. In 2016, Digital First sold several community newspaper groups in Alaska[54], Utah[55] and the Northeast[56] to local owners. In 2017, the company sold three Connecticut dailies and eight weeklies to Hearst. [57] The company has focused on regional consolidation within the markets where its other papers are located, such as combining eight San Francisco Bay-area newspapers into two titles in 2016 and laying off 20 percent of staff.[58] Most of the Digital First papers are located in California (76), followed by Pennsylvania (29) and Colorado (16).

According to the leaked financial statements, Digital First newspapers brought in $939 million in revenue in 2017 and had an operating income of $159 million.[59] This compares to GateHouse, the largest newspaper chain in the country, which had $1.3 billion in revenues in 2017 and an operating income of only $34.6 million.[60] Other large chains, including Gannett[61], and tronc/Tribune[62], also posted single digit margins in 2017. The higher margins posted by Digital First were the result of aggressive cost reductions at the newspapers, including multiple rounds of layoffs, and a lack of investment in both tangible assets, such as property and equipment, and intangible ones, such as wage increases to attract and retain talent. Reporters in two Philadelphia suburban newsrooms must work remotely because the Pottstown Mercury's mold-infested newspaper building has been condemned.[63] According to a poll of NewsGuild representatives at 12 Digital First papers,[64] staffing dropped 52 percent from 1,766 to 849 between 2012 and 2017. By comparison, between 2012 and 2016, the Bureau

DIGITAL FIRST MEDIA 2017 FINANCIAL RESULTS

Revenue (2017)	$939 mil	Operating Expenses	$780 mil
Digital Revenue	Unreported	Operating Income	$159 mil
Percent of Revenue From Digital	Unreported	Operating Margin	17%

SOURCE: Ken Doctor, "Newsonomics: Alden Global Capital is making so much money wrecking local journalism it might not want to stop anytime soon," Nieman Lab, May 1, 2018, http://www.niemanlab.org/2018/05/newsonomics-alden-global-capital-is-making-so-much-money-wrecking-local-journalism-it-might-not-want-to-stop-anytime-soon/"

of Labor Statistics estimates that total newspaper employment dropped by slightly more than a quarter overall.[65] The remaining staffers have been expected to work long hours without significant wage increases. "What sets (Alden president Heath) Freeman apart is that he seems to have a rather unique view of a newspaper's purpose," Bloomberg columnist Joe Nocera wrote in an editorial. "In this view, his papers are intended not so much to inform the public or hold officialdom to account, but to supply cash to use elsewhere. His layoffs aren't just painful. They are savage." [66]

As for the current financial sustainability of Digital First's strategy, the company has a $225 million loan that comes due in 2018, according to the Solus lawsuit. In a transcript of a June 2018 meeting between company executives and employees at the Denver Post Digital First chairman Joe Fuchs said the company has explored refinancing, but "the bond market has moved away from us. . .. The balance sheet of (Digital First) is as strong as you could possibly want it to be. . .. There's zero, zero financial vulnerability." [67]

The unrest across its newsrooms has prompted journalists and concerned community members to explore buying Digital First papers in several communities. This includes a Colorado civic group that has raised $10 million from local and statewide investors in an attempt to buy back the Denver Post, as well as similar efforts by editors and union representatives in California and the Philadelphia suburbs. [68] Digital First will reportedly entertain any offer at a minimum of 4 times earnings.[69]

However, based on the recent experience of local investors who have purchased Digital First papers, these new owners may struggle to return these

gutted and demoralized newsrooms to their former glory. When billionaire John Huntsman Sr. purchased the Salt Lake Tribune from Digital First in 2016, he told the staff that the family was prepared to devote money and work for "five, ten, fifteen years bringing back the great Salt Lake Tribune of yesterday." [70] However, after his death in February 2018, his son, Tribune publisher Paul Huntsman, laid off more than one-third of the newsroom's 90 employees. The Huntsman family had put more than $1 million into developing a new web production system and upgrading the Tribune's digital offerings, but in the two years since acquiring The Tribune, ad revenue had fallen by 40 percent and weekday circulation had dropped from 85,000 to under 31,000. In announcing the layoffs, Paul Huntsman said he had personally covered the "losses" at the paper for eight months, but concluded that without significant cost reductions, the financial picture of the paper was "not sustainable." [71]

In 2016, another group of four local investors purchased The Berkshire Eagle in Massachusetts and three nearby Vermont papers from Digital First. The investors immediately added staff and invested in website improvements and upgrades. "We thought that if we make these papers better than they were and return them to what they used to be, that will attract more readers," New England Newspapers Inc.'s president and publisher Fredric Rutberg said. "I frankly thought that we would get a lot of lapsed readers, people who got frustrated with what had happened in the previous five to ten years." Two years in, print circulation has stabilized, but there has not been a dramatic uptick. The investors say they remain committed to improving the newspapers, but concede they have had to temper their initial optimism, based on the financial realities they are confronting.[72]

Across the country, in Denver, a group including roughly a dozen former Post employees are trying another approach. Instead of attempting to buy the Post, they've decided to create a digital competitor.[73] Called the Colorado Sun, it uses blockchain technology, which is intended to add transparency to the gathering and reporting of news. They have partnered with Civil Media Company, a New York start-up that aspires to establish 1,000 local digital publications by the end of 2018.[74]

Yet, for all the heated rhetoric, picketing and news stories in the spring of 2018, it is business as usual at most Digital First newspapers. As one commentator put it, why would Alden Capital want to sell its papers when Digital First is achieving 17 percent margins? [75] This leaves community activists, journalists and potential investors still pondering the best way to revitalize the journalistic mission of the papers owned by Digital First. Should residents in the cities where the Digital First papers are located lobby Alden for change? Should they seek financing to purchase the paper? Or should they instead finance the start-up of a new print or digital publication to fill the void?

WHERE CNHI OWNS NEWSPAPERS: 2018

Frequency
- Daily
- Weekly

CNHI owns 114 newspapers in 21 states.
Source: UNC Database

CNHI: 114 papers in 2018

In the late 1990s, the portfolio managers of the Retirement Systems of Alabama (RSA) identified what they believed would be a worthwhile investment – regional broadcast stations and local newspapers in small and mid-sized markets, primarily in the South and Midwest. Instead of buying a minority stake in these companies, the Alabama state pension fund, known for its unorthodox investments in golf courses as well as a Manhattan skyscraper[76], decided to spend billions snapping up these newspapers and broadcast stations outright and then managing them on a day-to-day basis. [77]

RSA became one of the first investment funds to spot the earnings potential of newspapers and broadcasting operations in non-competitive markets, which often had operating margins of 20 to 50 percent in the pre-digital era. By 2004, its subsidiary, Community Newspaper Holdings Inc. (CNHI), was the fourth largest newspaper chain in the country, in terms of number of papers. It owned 149 papers, including 86 dailies, with an average circulation of less than 10,000.

However, the digital revolution and the 2008 recession changed the math for RSA, as margins – in even non-competitive markets – declined to single digits. The pension fund responded by expecting financial efficiency from all its newspapers, selling or closing those that were losing money, and, in the process, reducing the number of papers in its portfolio to 114. "We tried every way we could to keep the paper going, including talking to potential buyers," Steve McPhaul, CNHI executive vice president and chief operating officer, said of the 2014 closure of the Tarboro Daily Southerner in North Carolina, which, in its final days, had a circulation of less than 3,000. [78]

In late 2017, as the print revenue decline continued unabated, RSA decided to merge CNHI with Raycom Media, its broadcasting subsidiary, in an effort to further reduce costs, encourage digital collaboration between the two media groups, and decrease CNHI's reliance on print revenue.[79] "As always, we will continue to demand the best execution from all RSA counterparts, and will strive to produce results that strengthen the Retirement Systems of Alabama and its beneficiaries," the fund said in its 2017 annual report.[80] However, in June 2018, after only nine months, the marriage was dissolved. RSA announced that Gray Television had purchased Raycom for $3.6 billion. CNHI would be spun off [81] and its 114 newspapers – 73 dailies and 41 weeklies – sold.

The breakup comes at a tenuous time for CNHI. Its newspapers are circulated in 21 states; the dailies have an average circulation of 9,700, its weeklies, an average of 7,300 circulation. In the counties where CNHI owns newspapers, the average poverty rate is just over 17 percent—compared with the national average of less than 13 percent.[82] Even as it sold and shuttered papers, the company also made efforts to boost its journalism, designating a journalist in each state where it owned papers to cover statehouse news and produce regional enterprise stories.[83] To compensate for the added costs, the company cut back on staffing at individual papers and required remaining employees to take "furlough days" (days off without pay). [84] In an April 2018 interview with CNN on the company's plan for responding to increased tariffs on Canadian newsprint, CNHI president and CEO Donna Barrett said cutting staff isn't a "realistic option. . . We are already down to bare bones." Instead, she indicated the company would look at further reducing the number of pages in their newspapers or cutting print editions. [85]

Simultaneously, as profit margins decreased at CNHI, RSA has faced pressure to increase the return on its portfolio of investments. In 2001, the state pension plan was fully funded and had sufficient money to pay all its obligations. However, since then, investments made by RSA have repeatedly fallen short of expectations.[86] As a result, in 2015, Alabama faced $13 billion in state pension debts and another $11 billion in unfunded liabilities for retiree health insurance. This prompted an investigation by a government subcommittee. Over the past several years, the two boards that manage RSA have made efforts to curb the power of CEO David Bronner and expand oversight of the fund's investments. "We turned it from operating like a benevolent dictatorship to a democracy," then ERS (Employee Retirement Systems) board member James Rowell said in a 2015 interview. [87]

In 1997, right after RSA purchased Raycom and CNHI, the pension fund managed $21.6 million in assets and brought in $4.1 billion in revenue.[88] In 2017, RSA managed $41.5 billion in assets and brought in $6 billion in total revenue,[89] Raycom, which included CNHI, represented $2.9 billion of the pension fund's assets.[90] Bronner argues that while there have been some losing investments – such an oil rig repair firm that declared bankruptcy and was found liable for human trafficking[91] – his approach has led to significant growth for the pension fund.

RSA does not break out financial results for Raycom and CNHI, so it is not possible to track their year-over-year returns since 1997. CEO Bronner justified the acquisitions in the 1997 newsletter by saying, "The State of Alabama will receive approximately $26 million in advertising through Raycom Media and CNHI to promote various Alabama attractions from the Robert Trent Jones Golf Trail to the Space Camp." [92] In a December 2015 RSA newsletter, Bronner said the Raycom broadcasting division had a 16.4 percent annual rate of return. The return on the pension fund's entire portfolio that year was just over one percent.[93] In 2017, RSA's entire investment portfolio had a rate of return of more than 12 percent. But the pension fund still faces a shortfall. As of 2017, RSA's net pension liability, or the difference between its obligations and assets, totaled nearly $10 billion.[94]

In recent years, even as the newspapers struggled under worsening financial restraints, both the CNHI and Raycom divisions were reportedly covering the costs of the pension fund's corporate jets and pilots.[95] As a result, employee morale has suffered, as indicated by postings on recruiting and social media sites. "You could also provide the newsroom with enough staff to improve the quality and content of our products instead of adding more workload to the few employees that are left and not compensating them for the additional work required of them," a CNHI advertising employee said in an online job review. "If the only focus remains on the profit in your pocket and not on quality and content, you will continue to lose readership and advertisers."[96]

After the sale of Raycom to Gray, Bronner said in an RSA newsletter than the pension fund would have an 11 percent stake in the combined broadcast company with nearly $800 million invested into preferred and common stock. However, it would be ceding day-to-day management to Gray. Raycom will continue operating its headquarters in Montgomery, Alabama.[97]

In contrast to other investment funds, which aggressively manage their portfolio of assets, quickly selling or closing underperforming newspapers, RSA has pursued a different strategy. Instead of buying and flipping, the Alabama pension fund aimed to buy and hold its small papers, assuming they would generate steady and reliable returns for their retiree shareholders. But the digital revolution and the 2008 recession interceded, dramatically depressing margins. Like the readers and advertisers who abandoned the CNHI papers in recent years, RSA has decided to shed its newspaper habit. Once the CNHI newspapers are either sold — or closed if a buyer cannot be found — RSA will effectively conclude 20 years of media stewardship.

TRONC / TRIBUNE

WHERE TRONC/TRIBUNE OWNS NEWSPAPERS: 2018

Frequency
- Daily
- Weekly

Tronc/Tribune owns 77 papers in eight states.
Source: UNC Database

Tronc/Tribune: 77 papers in 2018

It has been a tumultuous decade for tronc/Tribune, full of more plot twists and turns than a good spy novel. In the first act, which begins in 2007, the Tribune Company is purchased by billionaire real estate magnate Sam Zell. Before exiting, he takes the company private, saddling it with $13 billion in debt. He also brings in a cast of characters who disrupt the staid Midwestern business culture and court controversy with accusations of hostile work environments and mismanagement. The second act involves bankruptcy, a change in ownership, restructuring, relisting of the stock on the New York Stock Exchange, a split of the company's newspaper and broadcasting divisions and an acquisition

spree. Act three begins with the 2016 takeover by technology entrepreneur Michael Ferro.[98]

Ferro starts his tenure as Tribune's largest shareholder by fending off increasingly generous buyout offers from the publicly traded newspaper chain Gannett.[99] To assist with the resistance, Ferro brings in a new shareholder, biotech billionaire Patrick Soon-Shiong. With an ambitious plan to go digital, Ferro then renames the Tribune Publishing Company "tronc"—in all lower-case letters, short for "Tribune online content.[100] Late night comics have a field day with the new name, comparing it to the sound of a duck honking. Soon-Shiong's and Ferro's relationship rapidly sours as they feud for control.[101] Soon-Shiong leaves the board in

2017[102] but returns in the closing act to purchase the company's largest newspaper, The Los Angeles Times, along with several Southern California titles in the spring of 2018. Ferro leaves the company amid sexual misconduct allegations[103] but strikes a deal to sell his shares in tronc to a distant relative of the McCormick family, which had owned The Chicago Tribune for much of its history. But the deal to sell tronc falls through. [104] As the curtain falls, the company is rumored to be weighing offers from potential buyers, [105] including at least one from a private equity group and another from the publicly traded newspaper chain McClatchy.[106]

Since the Tribune newspapers were spun off from the broadcasting group in 2014, the division has struggled financially, despite ambitious strategies to transform the company through digital investment and acquisitions. Revenues have declined every year, dropping from $1.71 billion in 2014 to $1.52 billion in 2017.[107] Ferro hoped to move the company toward a new business model that integrated cutting edge technology such as artificial intelligence, which could be used to produce hundreds of videos per day. [108] He split tronc into two divisions, one for print revenue and the other for digital revenue. [109] But the company's digital revenues rose by only 2 percent to approximately $240 million between 2016 and 2017, while its digital expenditures rose. Tronc's digital revenues now comprise about 16 percent of overall revenues, more than competitor GateHouse but still behind digital leaders such as Gannett and potential purchaser McClatchy.[110]

The company has also sought to exact savings from its print properties by acquiring nearby newspapers and merging the newsroom and back-office functions. But it has faced pushback from the Department of Justice (DOJ). In 2016, the DOJ blocked tronc's planned purchase of the Orange County Register and Riverside Press-Enterprise on antitrust grounds. According to the department's complaint, tronc's Los Angeles Times and the Orange County Register together would account for 98 percent of newspaper sales in Orange County.[111] In 2017, the DOJ also opened an investigation into what eventually became tronc's failed attempt to buy the Chicago Sun-Times, which Ferro previously owned.[112] The sale would have given tronc ownership of both Chicago dailies. On the other hand, tronc successfully acquired and incorporated the Annapolis Gazette into the Baltimore Sun group of papers in 2014, and in May 2018, purchased the Virginian-Pilot in Norfolk, Virginia, which it will consolidate with the nearby Daily Press in Newport News.[113]

As tronc's revenues have declined, the company has turned to cost cutting to improve margins. But, despite labor costs falling by more than 15 percent since 2015, its operating margins have remained in the low single digits, ranging from 1.4 percent to 4.4 percent. In 2017, the company identified more than 220 positions that could be eliminated, many of those in its newsrooms. [114] In July 2018, newsroom staffing at the New York Daily News, which tronc acquired in 2017, was cut in half with the layoff of more than 40 employees. [115] This came on top of several rounds of layoffs at the Daily News prior to the sale, which had brought newsroom staffing down from several hundred journalists only a decade ago.

The layoffs and cost cutting prompted employees at two of the largest tronc newspapers to take the unprecedented step of voting in unions in 2018. Employees at the Los Angeles Times, which had a strong anti-union history stretching back more than a hundred years, voted in January 2018 to join the NewsGuild CWA. [116] "Having a union won't

TRONC/TRIBUNE 2017 FINANCIAL RESULTS

Revenue (2017)	$1.52 bil	Operating Expenses	$1.46 bil
Digital Revenue	$240 mil	Operating Income	$66.6 mil
Percent of Revenue From Digital	16%	Operating Margin	4%

SOURCE: 2017 tronc SEC 10-K annual report filing

stop layoffs, but we have a collective voice and the days of the newsroom passively standing by while corporate management did whatever they wanted are over," said Los Angeles Times reporter Bettina Boxall. [117] Despite a concerted campaign by tronc to discourage the union effort, 248 of the 292 journalists at the Times cast votes in favor of joining the guild, spurred by concerns over the paper's leadership, stagnant wages and workplace misconduct. In April, journalists at the Chicago Tribune announced they were also attempting to unionize, for the first time in the paper's 171-year history.

As the union efforts proceed, tronc is preparing the company for sale. With the purchase of the Los Angeles Times by Soon-Shiong, tronc/Tribune now has 77 papers in its portfolio, including 17 dailies, located in some of the country largest metro markets. It has a total circulation of nearly 2.5 million in eight states. The average circulation of its daily newspapers is 105,000; the average circulation of its weeklies, most of which are located in the suburbs surrounding metro areas, is 13,000.

Tronc has said it will use the $500 million in proceeds from the sale of the Los Angeles Times, San Diego Union-Tribune and associated weeklies to Soon-Shiong to pay down long-term debt. As of its latest quarter, its long-term debt is nearly $327 million, meaning tronc will have cash reserves remaining after the debt is paid off. [118] When Gannett considered purchasing tronc in 2016 – before the lenders got cold feet and Gannett pulled out – the two companies agreed on a price of $18.75 per share, a 150 percent premium over the $8 price. [119] In August 2018, tronc was trading at nearly $17 per share and had a market valuation of almost $600 million. According to news accounts, initial offers are expected to be in the $700 million range. Rumored buyers this time include:

- The Donerail Group, a newly formed private equity fund that is led by Will Wyatt. Wyatt previously led the activist hedge fund Starboard Value, which took a $16 million stake in tronc in 2016. [120] In 2017, the hedge fund invested more than $70 million in Tribune Media, which is the broadcasting division that was spun off in 2014.[121]According to Reuters, Donerail has secured financing and is in advanced negotiations for the deal.[122]

- McClatchy, a public newspaper chain that owns nearly 50 papers, and has prioritized digital revenue and cost cutting across its portfolio. In 2006, McClatchy also purchased a larger chain, paying $4.5 billion for Knight-Ridder. It quickly resold a dozen of the papers acquired in the Knight-Ridder deal[123] and may adopt a similar strategy with tronc/Tribune. An acquisition of tronc/Tribune would give McClatchy, which owns papers in Miami; Charlotte, North Carolina; and Sacramento, California; access to even larger markets including Chicago and New York without assuming any additional debt from tronc's recently cleared balance sheet.

- Giant private equity firm Apollo Global Management, which nearly acquired Digital First Media in 2015. This would be the company's first official foray into newspapers.[124] Apollo manages a vast portfolio of investments, generating more than $2.5 billion in revenue, including Chuck E Cheese's, Diamond Resorts International and Chisholm Oil and Gas.

- New Media/GateHouse, a subsidiary of Fortress Investments, owned by SoftBank. When asked by an analyst in a May 2018 earnings call if Fortress might be considering a tronc purchase, Softbank CEO Masayoshi Son said he had no direct knowledge, but that he wouldn't stop the purchase. "At SoftBank, we don't have a direct interest at all, but some of the companies that we acquired, which is Fortress and also investees of Fortress, have interest or have an ownership of local newspaper companies," Son said.[125] "As long as they're making a good performance, I don't have any intention to stop them."

Whatever the future may hold for tronc/Tribune properties, the name "tronc" is a historical footnote. The day Soon-Shiong assumed ownership of the Los Angeles Times, employees hung signs in the building with backslashes through the "tronc" logo. In his comments to the newsroom staff, Soon-Shiong agreed with the sentiment. "Let's put tronc in the trunk and we're done,"[126] he said. On Oct. 4, the board of directors announced the revival of the company's previous name, Tribune Publishing Company.

BH MEDIA

WHERE BH MEDIA AND LEE ENTERPRISES OWN NEWSPAPERS: 2018

BH Media and Lee Enterprises own 175 newspapers in 29 states.
Source: UNC Database

Owner
- BH Media Group
- Lee Enterprises

BH Media: 75 papers in 2018

Berkshire Hathaway shareholders didn't get a chance to toss newspapers onto a makeshift front porch at the company's 2018 annual meeting in May. The highly publicized event was canceled.[127] The newspaper toss had been added to the annual shareholder meeting in Omaha with great fanfare in 2012 when Berkshire Hathaway purchased the Media General newspaper chain. Over the years, such celebrities as Bill Gates competed to see who had the most accurate newspaper toss. Invariably, Berkshire Hathaway Chairman Warren Buffett, who had delivered newspapers as a teenager, won.

That experience as a "paper boy" sparked a lifelong passion and appreciation for the newspaper

industry. Buffett served more than two decades as a member of the Washington Post board of directors, famously advising Katharine Graham, and in 1977 made his first newspaper purchase, The Buffalo News.[128] So, when Media General decided to sell its newspaper empire in 2012 and focus solely on its broadcasting properties, Buffett was an eager bidder.

Despite the business challenges confronting local newspapers, he told Berkshire Hathaway shareholders that the price was right, given the depressed valuations of newspapers, selling for three to five times earnings. "(Vice chairman) Charlie (Munger) and I believe that papers delivering comprehensible and reliable information to tightly bound communities and having a sensible Internet strategy will remain viable for a long time," he wrote in the 2012 letter to his shareholders. [129]

One month after canceling the annual newspaper toss, the famed "Oracle of Omaha" admitted that Berkshire Hathaway had failed to "crack the code" on newspaper ownership. [130] He formally turned over day-to-day management of his six-year-old newspaper empire, BH Media, to Lee Enterprises, a 128-year-old newspaper chain with more than a hundred papers in the Midwest.[131]

At its peak, the revenue from BH Media's 75 newspapers represented less than one percent of the total $242 billion in revenue[132] in the Berkshire Hathaway portfolio, which includes insurance companies, railroads and financial services. In 2013, Buffett said he was targeting an after tax-return of 10 percent for the newspapers, which he believed would be achievable without significant cost cutting. That year, company executives reported that the newspaper unit was profitable and debt free, except for a legacy mortgage on an Omaha newspaper building.[133] However, as print advertising and circulation declined – and the BH Media newspapers failed to significantly increase digital revenue – the print publications increasingly relied on a variety of cost-cutting measures to achieve the targeted return. In a 2017 memo, then BH Media president and CEO Terry Kroeger said that "without cost reductions, some BH Media operations would not be profitable." [134] The company resorted to hiring and wage freezes, as well as targeted layoffs and buyouts, as the employee count dropped from 4,074[135] in 2013 to 3,719 by 2017.[136]

In a press release announcing that Berkshire Hathaway was bowing out of the newspaper business and handing over day-to-day management of its empire to Lee, [137] Buffett praised Lee's

financial performance. Although its revenues have declined in recent years, Lee has maintained one of the highest operating margins in the industry. In 2017, Lee had an operating income of $92.5 million and a margin of 16 percent.[138] Roughly 20 percent of Lee's $566.9 million revenue came from digital initiatives. "It is very difficult to see . . . .. how the print product survives over time," Buffett said during a question-and-answer session at Berkshire Hathaway's 2018 annual meeting, acknowledging that his 2012 assessment of the long-term viability of print newspapers had missed the mark.[139]

Like BH Media, Lee also operates newspapers in small to midsized markets, ranging from Billings, Montana, to St. Louis, Missouri, and Tucson, Arizona. The BH Media newspapers are located in 11 states, mostly in the South and Midwest and serve small markets such as Dothan, Alabama, and Hickory, North Carolina, as well as mid-sized cities such as Richmond, Virginia, and Omaha, Nebraska. The average circulation of its 33 dailies is 27,500, and its weeklies have an average circulation of 7,300.

The two companies both own papers in Iowa, Nebraska, New York and South Carolina, although Lee says the only overlapping news coverage is between the Omaha World-Herald and Lincoln Journal Star in Nebraska.[140] In recent years, Lee has merged papers in regional proximity to reduce expenses. For example, in 2008, the company merged the daily 5,000-circulation South Idaho Press and several weeklies into the Twin Falls, Idaho Times-News.[141] The company has also bought papers, such as The Dispatch Argus in Moline, Illinois, in 2017, to strengthen its foothold in a region.[142]

Berkshire Hathaway has placed some restrictions on Lee's management of its papers. For example, Lee

LEE ENTERPRISES 2017 FINANCIAL RESULTS

Revenue (2017)	$567 mill	Operating Expenses	$474 mill
Digital Revenue	$106 mill	Operating Income	$92.5 mill
Percent of Revenue from Digital	19%	Operating Margin	16%

SOURCE: 2017 Lee Enterprises annual report filing

cannot outsource printing or change publication days without BH Media approval. However, for the most part, Lee is free to manage BH newspapers as if they were owned by Lee. It can reduce staff to "be consistent" with its own standards without permission from BH Media.[143] Between 2014 and 2017, Lee company decreased its compensation expenses by 8.4 percent, or $19 million, by cutting 9 percent of its workforce, from 4,500[144] to 3,626[145]. If Lee can't boost BH Media's revenues, it has strong incentive to cut costs. According to the management contract, Lee receives an annual fixed fee of $5 million, plus one-third of profits over $34 million in the first two years, and one-half of those profits in the final three years.[146]

Some in the industry saw an irony in Buffett's willingness to hand over management of his papers to Lee. In 2012, when Lee filed for bankruptcy protection, Buffett purchased some of the outstanding loans, which converted to preferred stock, thereby putting Berkshire Hathaway ahead of other creditors if Lee ultimately failed.[147] However, Buffett increased Berkshire's stake in the company once it emerged from bankruptcy by refinancing $94 million of Lee's long-term debt.[148] Lee paid off its debt to Berkshire Hathaway[149] two years early in 2015, freeing up the company's cash flows, and, undoubtedly impressing Buffett.

In 2017, Lee's long-term debt was down to $496.4 million,[150] a decrease of almost 50 percent since it declared bankruptcy.[151] "(This agreement with Berkshire Hathaway) enables us to generate more cash flow, speed our debt reduction, enhance our industry leadership and further advance our abilities as we introduce our digital and print strategies at BH Media properties," Lee executive chairman Mary Junck said in a statement about the agreement.

In interviews and talks, Buffett often acknowledges that newspapers' "significance to society is enormous."[152] Although he failed to "crack the code" on a new business model for newspapers, Buffett is now betting that a hundred-year-old newspaper company can. "The publishing business is in transition, to be sure, but we remain positive about our future," said Junck. "Many print opportunities remain, and digital audiences and revenue continue to grow and flourish."[153]

CIVITAS MEDIA

DECLINE IN CIVITAS MEDIA NEWSPAPERS: 2018

Civitas Media has divested from more than 90 newspapers over the past four years.
Source: UNC Database

Status
■ Sold
■ Still Owned

Civitas Media: 4 papers in 2018

Despite having a portfolio of nearly a hundred newspapers just four years ago, Civitas Media has bought and flipped its way to a near exit from the industry. Nearly six years after it formed, the company has sold or closed all of its newspapers except for four – the Times-Leader in Wilkes-Barre, Pennsylvania, and its affiliated weeklies. [154]

The Civitas chain of papers was created in 2012 through a merger of four bankrupt or financially distressed media companies bought by private equity firm Versa Capital Management. [155] Those four media companies were Freedom Central, Heartland Publications, Impressions Media and Ohio Community Media. At its peak, Civitas owned 98

papers in 12 states in the South and Midwest. Sixty percent of the papers in the Civitas chain were in counties with higher than average poverty rates. Its entire portfolio of small-market newspapers had an average circulation of under 10,000.

Versa's focus is on purchasing distressed properties, streamlining operations and then selling the assets. "We buy the whole company and fix it and then sell it," Versa founder and CEO Gregory Segall said in a 2016 interview with Bloomberg News.[156] "We are buying companies that are experiencing some kind of transition, maybe it was an operating problem. Maybe it was a strategy problem, an industry problem [or] a raw materials, supply problem." The Versa formula for "fixing" its newspapers involved dramatic cost cuts and regional consolidation, as well as short-term revenue tactics, such as increasing print circulation and advertising rates instead of investing in digital transformation. [157] As a result, employees often complained that Civitas stripped newsrooms, as well as advertising and circulation departments, of resources in order to turn a profit. "During our transition with Civitas, our newspapers have lost the hometown dedication along with customer support due to pricing of subscriptions and retail advertising," a business development representative at the Troy Daily News in Ohio wrote on a job review website. [158]

The investment company also resorted to closures if papers didn't meet targets. In 2013, Civitas closed eight suburban weekly newspapers around Raleigh, North Carolina, and Dayton, Ohio.[159] "Our core business is focused on developing community news and information portals, in areas that are predominately rural and would not be served well otherwise," then Civitas CEO Michael Bush said in a statement about the closures.[160] However, in late 2015, Civitas closed the 128-year-old, 2,500 circulation, Chronicle,[161] which served residents of the rural South Carolina community of Cheraw. [162]

Civitas sold almost all of its papers in 2016 and 2017 to AIM Media (36), Champion Media (22), Boone Newspapers (4), and Hearst (3), all of which are privately owned and operated newspaper chains. Civitas first sold the Mount Airy (North Carolina) News – along with more than 20 other papers in North Carolina and South Carolina– to Champion Media, started by the former chief operating officer of Civitas.[163] Less than four months later, Champion resold the Mount Airy group of eight papers to Adams Publishing Group.[164] "I think it's safe to say our previous ownership was an investment group, whose primary function was to maximize short-term profits while setting up the sale of its assets, without too much regard for what happens two or three or five years down the road," [165] editor John Peters wrote in his column. While nearly three-quarters of the Civitas papers acquired by the AIM, Adams and Boone companies are located in impoverished counties, the new owners have stated their commitment to investing in both the papers and the communities where the papers are located.

Versa retains ownership of only one regional newspaper group in Pennsylvania. The rationale for retaining the Wilkes-Barre Times-Leader group is unclear since as its finances are not publicly available. Compared to the majority of papers formerly in the Civitas portfolio, the Wilkes-Barre newspaper group is located in a county with a sizeable population of more than 300,000 people. Since 2014, the Times-Leader's circulation has fallen from 40,000 to nearly 24,000, a 40 percent decline that exceeds the national average. Versa says it is investing in the paper's future, setting aside $1 million to improve the printing press, upgrade the production facility and hire additional staff in editorial, ad sales and circulation. [166] "Versa would not have approved a $1 million investment in upgrading the press and infrastructure, improving our website and hiring additional personnel in our ad sales, circulation and editorial teams (if it wasn't committed)," said Lior Yahalomi, Civitas Media's CEO, in the Times-Leader editorial. "The Times-Leader Media Group is a profitable business, and we are going to continue improving our content and service for our customers." However, since announcing the $1 million investment, Versa has moved the Times-Leader to a smaller office building and laid off employees from several departments. [167]

Reflecting on the sale of the Mount Airy News to Adams Publishing, editor John Peters concluded, "The business world is made up primarily of two camps. The first places an emphasis on short-term maximum profitability on assets it can then sell, with little regard for long-term sustained growth. The second takes that longer-term approach, building relationships and quality, emphasizing sustainable profits, growth and customer satisfaction." [168]

10/13 COMMUNICATIONS

DECLINE IN 10/13 COMMUNICATIONS NEWSPAPERS: 2018

Status
- Sold
- Still Owned

10/13 Communications has divested from more than 40 newspapers over the past four years.
Source: UNC Database

10/13 Communications (Tucson Local Media): 3 papers in 2018

The advertiser-first mentality of 10/13 Communication has left its mark on the more than 40 papers the company owned for several years before selling them to four different owners in 2016. At the beginning of 2016, 10/13 was the 20th largest owner of newspapers, with 45 papers in Arizona and Texas. By year's end, it had divested nearly all its holdings, retaining just three weeklies in the Tucson, Arizona, area under the subsidiary Tucson Local Media. The papers it sold included three dailies and 39 weeklies, located in and around Dallas, Houston and Phoenix.

The investment entity 10/13 Communications formed in 2009 as a partnership between 10K Investments and 13th Street Media, which is led by Randy Miller. In the industry, Miller is known as an advocate for his advertisers. He believes in beefing up the sales staff, while keeping newsroom staffing lean. "Our customer is the advertiser. Readers are our customers' customers," a leaked 2007 13th Street Media guidebook read. "Sales calls are the primary contributing factor toward sales, so it is clear that the top priority at all of our newspapers is the sales department."[169] According to the guidebook, the company's newsrooms "operate with a lean core of newsroom staff and contributors and wire services for efficiency." In a 2015 media kit for advertisers, 10/13 sees its selling points as delivering "local news to targeted communities… we deliver the customers you want, where you want…we deliver results you need and return on investment."[170]

When 10/13 acquired several papers including Inside Tucson Business in 2014, editor Mark Evans resigned as employees were forced to reapply for a shrunken number of jobs.[171] "As spelled out in the manager's guide, the customer was the advertiser, the news was just something to put around the ads," he wrote in a column. "The company wasn't selling an audience; it was selling to advertisers a cheap way to put their ads in front of middle-to-upper income suburban homes." [172]

Hearst Corporation, which has $10 billion in annual revenues, purchased more than half of the 10/13 portfolio, including 23 weeklies and one daily in the Houston suburbs. [173] At the Key Executives Mega-Conference in San Diego in early 2018, Mark Aldam, COO of Hearst and executive vice president of its newspaper division, discussed results at the Houston papers.[174] When the newspapers were purchased from 10/13 in 2016, he said, the chain was struggling with steep declines in print revenue and earnings. Even more worrisome, the papers had no significant digital revenue. At the one-year mark, the papers had experienced 17 percent growth in advertising revenue by "importing" the Hearst "go-to-market playbook" for the advertising staff. This increased ad revenue had generated funds that could be used to invest in local journalism, Aldam said. The 10/13 papers became, in essence, zoned editions of the Houston Chronicle. By strategically linking the papers to the metro paper, Hearst was able to achieve "synergistic benefits" immediately and get a positive return on its investment in only a year's time.

The other 10/13 papers in Texas – 14 weeklies in the Dallas suburbs – were sold to S.A.W. Advisors, whose president, Scott Wright, has extensive experience managing private equity-owned newspapers, including a position as publisher of American Community Newspapers. In a statement at the time of purchase, he said that 10/13 did "an outstanding job" and that he would retain a similar strategy. "The goal is to provide hyper-local editorial content," he said. [175] "Our primary focus will continue to be on local government, education and high school sports. Most importantly, we will grow our digital endeavors at this company." The four Phoenix-area 10/13 papers went to two separate local owners, Times Media Group[176] and Independent Newsmedia[177].

The company's remaining papers — the Explorer News, Marana News, and Tucson Weekly — represent what's left of the 10/13 portfolio. The Explorer News and Tucson Weekly have a combined circulation of more than 75,000[178]. As of July 2018, Tucson Local Media operates with a staff of five journalists and 23 employees overall, including six advertising executives.[179] Because 10/13 is privately held, its financials on these newspapers are not publicly available.

Since the sale, 10/13 has made no statements or comments as to why it is retaining three papers in Arizona. As with its investment counterpart, Civitas Media, which exited the market except for one newspaper group in Pennsylvania, the company may own these papers for the foreseeable future, or it may be prepping them for another sale.

Research Assistant Alex Dixon compiled data and did much of the analysis in this report. He is a researcher in the Center for Innovation and Sustainability in Local Media in the School of Media and Journalism at the University of North Carolina at Chapel Hill.

CITATIONS

1   Thomas Gnau, "Company to close three Dayton-area papers," Dayton Daily News, July 18, 2013, https://www.daytondailynews.com/business/company-close-three-dayton-area-papers/IIGcTduOtl98nNBctkDZTI/

2   Ken Doctor, "Newsonomics: GateHouse's Mike Reed talks about rolling up America's news industry" Nieman Journalism Lab, June 20, 2018 http://www.niemanlab.org/2018/06/newsonomics-gatehouses-mike-reed-talks-about-rolling-up-americas-news-industry/?utm_source=Daily+Lab+email+list&utm_campaign=ab68544c9e-dailylabemail3&utm_medium=email&utm_term=0_d68264fd5e-ab68544c9e-396186933

3   Pew Research Center analysis of Bureau of Labor Statistics Occupational Employment Statistics data, June 13, 2018, http://www.journalism.org/fact-sheet/newspapers/

4   Julie Reynolds, "Working under a hedge fund: how billionaires made the crisis at America's news papers even worse," dfmworkers.org, April 10, 2017, https://dfmworkers.org/working-under-a-hedge-fund-how-billionaires-made-the-crisis-at-americas-newspapers-even-worse/

5   Joe Nocera, "Alden Global Capital's Business Model Destroys Newspapers for Little Gain," Bloomberg, March 26, 2018, https://www.bloomberg.com/view/articles/2018-03-26/alden-global-capital-s-business-model-destroys-newspapers-for-little-gain

6   Ken Doctor, "Newsonomics: Alden Global Capital is making so much money wrecking local journalism it might not want to stop anytime soon," Nieman Lab, May 1, 2018, http://www.niemanlab.org/2018/05/newsonomics-alden-global-capital-is-making-so-much-money-wrecking-local-journalism-it-might-not-want-to-stop-anytime-soon/

7   GateHouse Center for News and Design, 2018, http://www.centerfornewsanddesign.com/

8   "GateHouse names new publisher for group of 8 Ohio Newspapers, Associated Press, April 5, 2017, https://www.usnews.com/news/best-states/ohio/articles/2017-04-05/gatehouse-names-new-publisher-for-group-of-8-ohio-newspapers

9   Leia Parker, Bryce Druzin, "Bay Area News Group consolidates newspapers in Silicon Valley, Easy Bay and on the Peninsula," Silicon Valley Business Journal, March 1, 2016, https://www.bizjournals.com/sanjose/news/2016/03/01/bay-area-news-group-consolidates-newspapers-in.html

10   New Media Investment Group, Company Overview, Q1 2018, May 3, 2018, http://ir.newmediainv.com/Presentations

11   "What Investment Companies Say About Themselves," Center for Innovation and Sustainability in Local Media, University of North Carolina at Chapel Hill, 2016, http://newspaperownership.com/additional-material/investment-newspaper-owners-statements/

12   Steve Henson. "GateHouse, Rawlings reach deal on sale of The Pueblo Chieftain" The Pueblo Chieftain May 8 2018, https://www.chieftain.com/news/pueblo/gatehouse-rawlings-reach-deal-on-sale-of-the-pueblo-chieftain/article_17de5ed6-5548-5fde-bc7e-fca5e349a08a.html

13   Circulation from Alliance for Audited Media

14   Research correspondence with Pueblo Chieftain Journalist and Union Representative Luke Lyons

15   New Media Investment Group, Company Overview, Q1 2018, May 3, 2018, http://ir.newmediainv.com/Presentations

16   Frank Morris, "Can A New Business Model Save Small-Town Papers?" National Public Radio, May 8 2018, https://www.npr.org/2018/05/08/609304180/can-a-new-business-model-save-small-town-papers
     See also: Tiffany Eckert, "What Eugene, OR And Columbia, MO Have In Common: GateHouse Media," KLCC, June 14, 2018, http://www.klcc.org/post/what-eugene-or-and-columbia-mo-have-common-gatehouse-media

17   Terry Ganey, "The Tribune's "Tragedy," Gateway Journalism Review, February 21, 2018, http://gatewayjr.org/2018/02/21/the-tribunes-tragedy/

18   New Media Investment Group, Annual Report 2017, February 28, 2018

19   New Media Investment Group, Annual Report 2017, February 28, 2018
      See also: New Media Investment Group, Company Overview, Q1 2018, May 3, 2018, http://ir.newme-diainv.com/Presentations

20   Gary Dinges. "Statesman to end Ahora Sí, offer voluntary severance to all employees," Austin American-Statesman, August 9, 2018, https://www.statesman.com/business/statesman-end-ahora-offer-voluntary-severance-all-employees/tENrq1FeHfgoAIe9hNeGRM/

21   New Media Investment Group, "GateHouse Media, Inc. Completes Restructuring and Emerges from Chapter 11," November 26, 2013, https://www.prnewswire.com/news-releases/gatehouse-media-inc-completes-restructuring-and-emerges-from-chapter-11-233494921.html

22   New Media Investment Group, Annual Report 2017, February 28, 2018

23   Ken Doctor, "Newsonomics: GateHouse's Mike Reed talks about rolling up America's news industry" Nieman Journalism Lab, June 20, 2018 http://www.niemanlab.org/2018/06/newsonomics-gatehouses-mike-reed-talks-about-rolling-up-americas-news-industry/?utm_source=Daily+Lab+email+list&utm_campaign=ab68544c9e-dailylabemail3&utm_medium=email&utm_term=0_d68264fd5e-ab68544c9e-396186933

24   SoftBank Group's (SFTBF) CEO Masayoshi Son on Q4 2017 Results - Earnings Call Transcript, Seeking Alpha, May 10, 2018, https://seekingalpha.com/article/4172636-softbank-groups-sftbf-ceo-masayoshi-son-q4-2017-results-earnings-call-transcript?part=single

25   New Media Investment Group, Company Overview, Q1 2018, May 3, 2018, http://ir.newmediainv.com/Presentations

26   Ken Doctor, "Newsonomics: GateHouse's Mike Reed talks about rolling up America's news industry" Nieman Journalism Lab, June 20, 2018 http://www.niemanlab.org/2018/06/newsonomics-gatehouses-mike-reed-talks-about-rolling-up-americas-news-industry/?utm_source=Daily+Lab+email+list&utm_campaign=ab68544c9e-dailylabemail3&utm_medium=email&utm_term=0_d68264fd5e-ab68544c9e-396186933

27   UNC 2018 Database, Center for Innovation and Sustainability in Local Media

28   Circulation from Alliance for Audited Media

29   New Media Investment Group, Annual Report 2017, February 28, 2018

30   Gannett, Annual Report 2017, February 20, 2018

31   Ken Doctor, "Newsonomics: GateHouse's Mike Reed talks about rolling up America's news industry" Nieman Journalism Lab, June 20, 2018 http://www.niemanlab.org/2018/06/newsonomics-gatehouses-mike-reed-talks-about-rolling-up-americas-news-industry/?utm_source=Daily+Lab+email+list&utm_campaign=ab68544c9e-dailylabemail3&utm_medium=email&utm_term=0_d68264fd5e-ab68544c9e-396186933

32   Edited Transcript of NEWM earnings conference call or presentation, February 28, 2018 https://finance.yahoo.com/news/edited-transcript-newm-earnings-conference-034603362.html

33   Frank Morris, "Can A New Business Model Save Small-Town Papers?" National Public Radio, May 8 2018, https://www.npr.org/2018/05/08/609304180/can-a-new-business-model-save-small-town-papers

34   Gerry Smith, "The Hard Truth at Newspapers Across America: Hedge Funds Are in Charge", Bloomberg News, May 22, 2018, https://www.bloomberg.com/news/articles/2018-05-22/the-hard-truth-at-newspapers-across-america-hedge-funds-are-in-charge

35   Florida Times-Union Newsroom Employees Formally Kick Off Unionizing Drive, Florida NewsGuild, June 19, 2018, https://www.editorandpublisher.com/news/florida-times-union-newsroom-employees-formally-kick-off-unionizing-drive/

36   New Media Investment Group, Annual Report 2017, February 28, 2018

37   "Guild Reaches First-of-its-Kind Agreement with GateHouse," The NewsGuild, Communications Workers of America, December 15, 2017, http://www.newsguild.org/mediaguild3/guild-reaches-first-of-its-kind-agreement-with-gatehouse/

38   Stephen Franklin, "The Chicago Tribune Is Finally Union as the Media Organizing Wave Intensifies," In These Times, June 4, 2018, http://inthesetimes.com/working/entry/21182/chicago_tribune_union_labor_media_tronc_newsguild

39   UNC 2018 Database, Center for Innovation and Sustainability in Local Media

40   Terry Ganey, "The Tribune's "Tragedy," Gateway Journalism Review, February 21, 2018, http://gatewayjr.org/2018/02/21/the-tribunes-tragedy/

41   Charles Westmoreland, "Editor's Corner: Let's talk about the Tribune," Columbia Daily Tribune , December 1, 2017, http://www.columbiatribune.com/news/20171201/editors-corner-lets-talk-about-tribune

42   Julie Reynolds, "Hedge fund Alden siphoned 100s of millions from newspapers in scheme to gamble on other investments, suit says," dfmworkers.org, March 8, 2018 https://dfmworkers.org/hedge-fund-alden-siphoned-100s-of-millions-from-newspapers-in-scheme-to-gamble-on-other-investments-suit-says/

43   Ken Doctor, "Newsonomics: Alden Global Capital is making so much money wrecking local journalism it might not want to stop anytime soon," Nieman Lab, May 1, 2018, http://www.niemanlab.org/2018/05/newsonomics-alden-global-capital-is-making-so-much-money-wrecking-local-journalism-it-might-not-want-to-stop-anytime-soon/

44   Circulation from Alliance for Audited Media

45   Joe Nocera, "Alden Global Capital's Business Model Destroys Newspapers for Little Gain," Bloomberg, March 26, 2018, https://www.bloomberg.com/view/articles/2018-03-26/alden-global-capital-s-business-model-destroys-newspapers-for-little-gain

46   John Wenzel, "The Denver Post and the Future of Local News," The Atlantic, May 11, 2018 https://www.theatlantic.com/entertainment/archive/2018/05/denver-post/560186/?utm_source=API+Need+to+Know+newsletter&utm_campaign=3a0dff6201-EMAIL_CAMPAIGN_2018_05_14&utm_medium=email&utm_term=0_e3bf78af04-3a0dff6201-45841509

47   Corey Hutchins, "From the rubble, The Denver Post's editorial board rebuilds. Differently," The Colorado Independent, August 31, 2018, https://www.coloradoindependent.com/2018/08/31/denver-post-editorial-board-colorado-media/

48   Ravi Somaiya, "Lofty Newspaper Project Is Closed After Two Years," New York Times, April 2, 2014, https://www.nytimes.com/2014/04/03/business/media/lofty-newspaper-project-is-closed-after-two-years.html

49   Ken Doctor, "Apollo withdraws from D.F.M. deal, Paton leaves," POLITICO, May 14, 2015, https://www.politico.com/media/story/2015/05/apollo-withdraws-from-dfm-deal-paton-leaves-003777

50   Beau Yarbrough, "Attorney: Freedom Communications to sell to Digital First Media – Daily News," Los Angeles Daily News, March 19, 2016 https://www.dailynews.com/2016/03/19/attorney-freedom-communications-to-sell-to-digital-first-media/

51   Tracey Lien, "OC Register and other Digital First Media newspapers face 'significant' layoffs," Los Angeles Times, January 15, 2018 http://www.latimes.com/business/technology/la-fi-tn-ocr-layoffs-20180115-story.html

52   Circulation from Alliance for Audited Media

53   Nik DeCosta-Klipa, "Inside the 'dehumanizing' cost-cutting efforts by new ownership at the Boston Herald," Boston.com, May 15, 2018, https://www.boston.com/news/media/2018/05/15/boston-herald-digital-first-media

54   Weston Morrow, "Helen E. Snedden Foundation expands mission with News-Miner purchase," Fairbanks Daily News-Miner, December 22, 2015, http://www.newsminer.com/news/local_news/helen-e-snedden-foundation-expands-mission-with-news-miner-purchase/article_e87c8aaa-a952-11e5-ad1f-63ae627d93f5.html

55   Karissa Neely, "Digital First Media to sell The Salt Lake Tribune to Paul Huntsman," Daily Herald, April 20, 2016, https://www.heraldextra.com/business/local/digital-first-media-to-sell-the-salt-lake-tribune-to/article_d24e132d-b065-5769-ba10-9205632083f3.html

56   Clarence Fanto, "The Bennington Banner returning to local ownership," Bennington Banner, April 21, 2016, https://www.benningtonbanner.com/stories/the-bennington-banner-returning-to-local-ownership,105919

57   "Hearst Acquires Print, Digital and Local Media Assets of 21st Century Media Newspaper, LLC, Including the New Haven Register," June 5, 2017, http://www.hearst.com/newsroom/hearst-acquires-print-digital-and-local-media-assets-of-21st-century-media-newspaper-llc-including-the-new-haven-register

58   Marissa Lang, "Oakland loses Tribune, with paper folded into new East Bay Times," San Francisco Chronicle, March 1, 2016, https://www.sfgate.com/business/article/Bay-Area-News-Group-consolidates-newspapers-6863720.php

59   Ken Doctor, "Newsonomics: Alden Global Capital is making so much money wrecking local journalism it might not want to stop anytime soon," Nieman Lab, May 1, 2018, http://www.niemanlab.org/2018/05/newsonomics-alden-global-capital-is-making-so-much-money-wrecking-local-journalism-it-might-not-want-to-stop-anytime-soon/

60   New Media Investment Group, Annual Report 2017, February 28, 2018

61   Gannett, Annual Report 2017, February 20, 2018

62   Tronc, 2017 Annual Report, March 16, 2018

63   Bob Fernandez," Digital First Media closes mold-ridden Pottstown Mercury building," Philadelphia Inquirer, June 4, 2018, http://www2.philly.com/philly/business/digital-first-media-closes-pottstown-mercury-mold-alden-capital-20180604.html

64   Julie Reynolds, "Working under a hedge fund: how billionaires made the crisis at America's newspapers even worse," dfmworkers.org, April 10, 2017, https://dfmworkers.org/working-under-a-hedge-fund-how-billionaires-made-the-crisis-at-americas-newspapers-even-worse/

65   "Newspaper publishers lose over half their employment from January 2001 to September 2016," Bureau of Labor Statistics, April 3, 2017, https://www.bls.gov/opub/ted/2017/newspaper-publishers-lose-over-half-their-employment-from-january-2001-to-september-2016.htm?mc_cid=e73bf40429&mc_eid=c1d0b252cf

66   Joe Nocera, "Alden Global Capital's Business Model Destroys Newspapers for Little Gain," Bloomberg, March 26, 2018, https://www.bloomberg.com/view/articles/2018-03-26/alden-global-capital-s-business-model-destroys-newspapers-for-little-gain

67   Julie Reynolds, "Showtime in Denver: an annotated transcript," dfmworkers.org, June 22, 2018, https://dfmworkers.org/showtime-in-denver-an-annotated-transcript/

68   Sydney Ember, "Colorado Group Pushes to Buy Embattled Denver Post From New York Hedge Fund," The New York Times, April 12, 2018 https://www.nytimes.com/2018/04/12/business/media/denver-post-alden-global-capital.html

69   Ken Doctor, "Newsonomics: Alden Global Capital is making so much money wrecking local journalism it might not want to stop anytime soon," Nieman Lab, May 1, 2018, http://www.niemanlab.org/2018/05/newsonomics-alden-global-capital-is-making-so-much-money-wrecking-local-journalism-it-might-not-want-to-stop-anytime-soon/

70   Rick Edmonds, "High hopes dashed — why The Salt Lake Tribune fell so far so fast," Poynter, May 25, 2018, https://www.poynter.org/news/high-hopes-dashed-why-salt-lake-tribune-fell-so-far-so-fast

71   Tony Semerad, "The Salt Lake Tribune faces layoffs, cuts to print offerings," The Salt Lake Tribune, May 8, 2018, https://www.sltrib.com/news/2018/05/08/the-salt-lake-tribune-facing-layoffs-cuts-to-print-offerings/

72   Research Interview with New England Newspapers Inc. president Fredric Rutberg, July 13, 2018

73   Corey Hutchins, "The Denver Post's politics desk implodes. Three of its team will write for The Sun," Colorado Independent, July 20, 2018, https://www.coloradoindependent.com/2018/07/20/denver-post-colorado-sun-politics/

74   Jaclyn Peiser, "Goodbye, Denver Post. Hello, Blockchain." New York Times, June 17, 2018, https://www.nytimes.com/2018/06/17/business/media/denver-post-blockchain-colorado-sun.html

75   Ken Doctor, "Newsonomics: Alden Global Capital is making so much money wrecking local journalism it might not want to stop anytime soon," Nieman Lab, May 1, 2018, http://www.niemanlab.org/2018/05/newsonomics-alden-global-capital-is-making-so-much-money-wrecking-local-journalism-it-might-not-want-to-stop-anytime-soon/

76   William Thornton, "Retirement Systems of Alabama owns a Manhattan skyscraper? What else?," AL.com, July 5, 2018, https://www.al.com/expo/news/erry-2018/07/33106dfd659493/heres_a_few_of_the_retirement.html

77   Felicity Barringer, "Spreading the Small-Town News; A New Sort of Company Invests in Community Papers," The New York Times, May 31, 1999, https://www.nytimes.com/1999/05/31/business/spreading-the-small-town-news-a-new-sort-of-company-invests-in-community-papers.html

See also: Joseph B. Treaster, "Venture in Accord to Buy 7 TV Stations From Aflac," The New York Times, August 14, 1996 https://www.nytimes.com/1996/08/14/business/venture-in-accord-to-buy-7-tv-stations-from-aflac.html

78   "Daily Southerner closes after 125-year run," Rocky Mount Telegram, May 31, 2014 http://www.rockymounttelegram.com/Tarboro/2014/05/31/Daily-Southerner-closes-after-125-year-run.html

79   "Raycom Media, CNHI Announce Merger ," Raycom Media, September 25, 2017, https://www.raycommedia.com/raycom-media-cnhi-announce-merger/

80   Retirement Systems of Alabama, Comprehensive Annual Financial Report 2017, January 31, 2018 https://www.rsa-al.gov/uploads/files/RSA_2017_CAFR.pdf

81   "CNHI explores sale of newspaper company," CNHI News Service, June 25, 2018, https://www.cnhi.com/company-news/cnhi-explores-sale-of-newspaper-company/article_0903bd50-7879-11e8-9307-8716402d0f8f.html

82   UNC 2018 Database, Center for Innovation and Sustainability in Local Media

83   Susannah Nesmith, State coverage gets a boost from local-focused media company, Columbia Journalism Review, December 9, 2015, https://www.cjr.org/united_states_project/state_coverage_gets_boost_from_local-focused_media_company.php

84   Matt Burke, "Boston Herald GateHouse update: What is the future for Herald?", Metro, December 10, 2017 https://www.metro.us/news/local-news/boston/boston-herald-gatehouse-update-what-the-future-herald

85   Jill Disis, "Local newspapers fear tariffs could cripple them," CNN Money, April 21, 2018, https://money.cnn.com/2018/04/21/media/newspaper-canada-tariffs/index.html

86   Greg Mennis, "How to strengthen Alabama's pension system for workers and taxpayers," AL.com, September 15, 2016, https://www.al.com/opinion/index.ssf/2016/09/how_to_strengthen_alabamas_pen.html
See also: James Barth, John Jahera, Alabama's Public Pensions, Building a Stable Financial Foundation for the Years Ahead, Alabama Policy Institute, 2015, https://www.rsa-al.gov/uploads/files/API_study_for_cash_balance_plan.pdf

87   Casey Toner, "RSA under fire: Inside the latest battle over Alabama's pension powerhouse," AL.com, September 24, 2015, https://www.al.com/news/index.ssf/2015/09/retirement_systems_of_alabama.html

88   Retirement Systems of Alabama, 1997 Annual Report, https://www.rsa-al.gov/uploads/files/Annual_Report_1997.pdf

89   Retirement Systems of Alabama, 2017 Annual Report, https://www.rsa-al.gov/uploads/files/2017_RSA_Annual_Report.pdf

90   Retirement Systems of Alabama, 2017 Annual Report, https://www.rsa-al.gov/uploads/files/2017_RSA_Annual_Report.pdf

91   Casey Toner, "RSA under fire: Inside the latest battle over Alabama's pension powerhouse," AL.com, September 24, 2015, https://www.al.com/news/index.ssf/2015/09/retirement_systems_of_alabama.html

92   Retirement Systems of Alabama, 1997 Annual Report, https://www.rsa-al.gov/uploads/files/Annual_Report_1997.pdf

93   Retirement Systems of Alabama, "The Advisor," December 2015, https://www.rsa-al.gov/uploads/files/Advisor_December_15.pdf

94   Retirement Systems of Alabama, Comprehensive Annual Financial Report 2017, January 31, 2018 https://www.rsa-al.gov/uploads/files/RSA_2017_CAFR.pdf

95   Cliff Sims, "How an Alabama state employee built a billionaire's lifestyle in a taxpayer-funded job (opinion)," Yellowhammer News, 2015, https://yellowhammernews.com/how-an-alabama-state-employee-built-billionaire-lifestyle/

96   "Community Newspaper Holdings Reviews," Glassdoor, August 11, 2017, https://www.glassdoor.com/Reviews/Community-Newspaper-Holdings-Reviews-E8583_P2.htm

97   Retirement Systems of Alabama, "The Advisor," August 2018, https://www.rsa-al.gov/uploads/files/Advisor_Aug_18_web.pdf

98 Timeline: Tribune's ownership saga, Chicago Tribune, June 18, 2018, http://www.chicagotribune.com/ct-history-of-tribune-ownership-saga-20160204-htmlstory.html

99 Gerry Smith, "Tribune Investor Seeks to Revive Print With 'Machine Vision'," Bloomberg, May 23, 2016, https://www.bloomberg.com/news/articles/2016-05-23/new-tribune-investor-seeks-to-revive-print-with-machine-vision

100 Erik Wemple, "Tribune Publishing, now 'tronc,' issues worst press release in the history of journalism, The Washington Post, June 2, 2016, https://www.washingtonpost.com/blogs/erik-wemple/wp/2016/06/02/tribune-co-now-tronc-issues-worst-press-release-in-the-history-of-journalism/?noredirect=on&utm_term=.25c10475fd3e

101 Sydney Ember, "Tronc Feud Escalates as Billionaire Investor Demands Access to Records," The New York Times, March 27, 2017, https://www.nytimes.com/2017/03/27/business/media/tronc-patrick-soon-shiong-ferro-nant.html

102 Douglas Mcintyre, "Tronc Vice Chair Soon-Shiong to Leave Board," 24/7 Wall Street, March 20, 2017, https://247wallst.com/media/2017/03/20/tronc-vice-chair-soon-shiong-to-leave-board/

103 Robert Channick, Michael Ferro steps down as Tronc chairman hours before sexual misconduct allegations published," Chicago Tribune, March 20, 2018, http://www.chicagotribune.com/business/ct-biz-ferro-retires-tronc-chairman-20180319-story.html

104 "History of Tribune ownership saga," Chicago Tribune, June 18, 2018 http://www.chicagotribune.com/ct-history-of-tribune-ownership-saga-20160204-htmlstory.html

105 Brooke Sutherland, Tronc in Play: Apollo, Gannett May Buy All or Pieces," Bloomberg, April 16, 2018 https://www.bloomberg.com/gadfly/articles/2018-04-16/tronc-in-play-apollo-gannett-may-buy-all-or-pieces

106 Robert Channick, "Chicago Tribune's owner considering bid for company, sources say," Chicago Tribune, August 8, 2018 http://www.chicagotribune.com/business/ct-biz-tronc-newspapers-offer-20180808-story.html
See also: Robert Channick, "Tronc in 'early stage' discussions about sale to McClatchy newspaper chain," September 15, 2018, https://www.latimes.com/business/la-fi-tronc-mcclatchy-20180915-story.html

107 Tronc 2017 annual report, March 7, 2018

108 Felix Gillette, Gerry Smith, "Tronc If You Want to Save Journalism," Bloomberg, November 2, 2016 https://www.bloomberg.com/features/2016-tronc/

109 Peter Sterne, "Tronc restructures into traditional and digital publishing units," POLITICO, August 3, 2016, https://www.politico.com/media/story/2016/08/tronc-restructures-into-traditional-and-digital-publishing-units-004697

110 Tronc 2017 annual report, March 7, 2018

111 Department of Justice, "Justice Department Files Antitrust Lawsuit to Stop L.A. Times Publisher from Acquiring Competing Newspapers," March 17, 2016, https://www.justice.gov/opa/pr/justice-department-files-antitrust-lawsuit-stop-la-times-publisher-acquiring-competing

112 Department of Justice, "Department of Justice Statement on the Closing of Its Investigation into the Possible Acquisition of Chicago Sun-Times by Owner of Chicago Tribune," July 12, 2017, https://www.justice.gov/opa/pr/department-justice-statement-closing-its-investigation-possible-acquisition-chicago-sun-times

113 Tara Bozick, "Virginian-Pilot sold to Tronc, parent company of the Daily Press," Daily Press, May 29, 2018, http://www.dailypress.com/news/dp-nws-tronc-virginian-pilot-20180529-story.html

114 Tronc 2017 annual report, March 7, 2018

115 Jaclyn Peiser, "Daily News Newsroom Cut in Half by Tronc as Top Editor Is Ousted," The New York Times, July 23, 2018 https://www.nytimes.com/2018/07/23/business/media/tronc-daily-news-layoffs.html

116 Stephen Franklin, "The Chicago Tribune Is Finally Union as the Media Organizing Wave Intensifies," In These Times, June 4, 2018, http://inthesetimes.com/working/entry/21182/chicago_tribune_union_labor_media_tronc_newsguild

117 Dave Jamieson, Ann Brenoff, Matt Ferner, Maxwell Strachan, "How The LA Times Union Won," HuffPost, January 19, 2018, https://www.huffingtonpost.com/entry/los-angeles-times-union-won_us_5a626c2fe4b0e563006fa774

118   Robert Channick, "Tronc set to complete $500 million LA Times sale to biotech billionaire Monday," Chicago Tribune, June 16, 2018, http://www.chicagotribune.com/business/ct-biz-tronc-closes-la-times-sale-20180616-story.html

119   Lukas Alpert, Dana Cimilluca, Joshua Jamerson, "Gannett Ends Its Attempt to Buy Chicago Tribune Publisher Tronc," Wall Street Journal, November 1, 2016, https://www.wsj.com/articles/gannett-abandons-its-attempt-to-buy-tronc-1478004408

120   Securities and Exchange Commission, Form 13F, 2016 https://www.sec.gov/Archives/edgar/data/1517137/000092189516006097/xslForm13F_X01/info table.xml

121   Securities and Exchange Commission, Form 13F, 2017 https://www.sec.gov/Archives/edgar/data/1517137/000092189517000382/xslForm13F_X01/info table.xml

122   Greg Roumeliotis, "Exclusive: Donerail Group in talks to buy Chicago Tribune owner Tronc – sources," Reuters, August 9, 2018, https://www.reuters.com/article/us-tronc-m-a-donerail-exclusive/exclusive-donerail-group-in-talks-to-buy-chicago-tribune-owner-tronc-sources-idUSKBN1KU28V

123   Jim Romenesko, "McClatchy buys Knight-Ridder, will sell 12 KR newspapers," Poynter, March 13, 2006, https://www.poynter.org/news/mcclatchy-buys-knight-ridder-will-sell-12-kr-newspapers

124   Brooke Sutherland, Tronc in Play: Apollo, Gannett May Buy All or Pieces," Bloomberg, April 16, 2018 https://www.bloomberg.com/gadfly/articles/2018-04-16/tronc-in-play-apollo-gannett-may-buy-all-or-pieces

125   "SoftBank Group's (SFTBF) CEO Masayoshi Son on Q4 2017 Results - Earnings Call Transcript," Seeking Alpha, May 9, 2018 https://seekingalpha.com/article/4172636-softbank-groups-sftbf-ceo-masayoshi-son-q4-2017-results-earnings-call-transcript?part=single

126   Meg James, Andrea Chang, "New Los Angeles Times owner Patrick Soon-Shiong names veteran journalist Norman Pearlstine executive editor," Los Angeles Times, June 18, 2018, http://www.latimes.com/business/hollywood/la-fi-ct-norman-pearlstine-latimes-editor-20180618-story.html

127   Steve Jordon, "Shareholders won't be tossing newspapers at this year's Berkshire Hathaway meeting," Omaha World-Herald, April 13, 2018 https://www.omaha.com/money/shareholders-won-t-be-tossing-newspapers-at-this-year-s/article_9a9b2a84-9dfd-5638-bc39-3d27b7b4ffe8.html

128   Berkshire Hathaway, Annual Shareholder Letter, 2012, http://www.berkshirehathaway.com/letters/2012ltr.pdf

129   Berkshire Hathaway, Annual Shareholder Letter, 2012, http://www.berkshirehathaway.com/letters/2012ltr.pdf

130   Rem Rieder, "Newspapers haven't 'cracked code,' Buffett says," USA Today, May 25, 2016, https://www.usatoday.com/story/money/columnist/rieder/2016/05/25/rieder-newspapers-havent-cracked-code-buffett-says/84902818/

131   "Lee Enterprises will manage Berkshire Hathaway newspaper and digital operations in 30 markets," Lee Enterprises, June 26, 2018 http://lee.net/financial/lee-enterprises-will-manage-berkshire-hathaway-newspaper-and-digital-operations/article_ebb48fee-78d3-11e8-a3a5-1fc0f14b0847.html

132   Berkshire Hathaway, 2017 Annual Report, February 24, 2018

133   Anupreeta Das, "At Papers, Berkshire Rewrites Its Script," Wall Street Journal, January 2, 2014, https://www.wsj.com/articles/at-papers-berkshire-rewrites-its-script-1388615859

134   Steve Jordon, "BH Media cuts 289 jobs; none are at World-Herald," Omaha World-Herald, April 4, 2017, https://www.omaha.com/money/bh-media-cuts-jobs-none-are-at-world-herald/article_8d721112-18ae-11e7-b90e-278b2db14b52.html

135   Berkshire Hathaway, 2014 Annual Report, February 27, 2015,

136   Berkshire Hathaway, 2017 Annual Report, February 24, 2018

137   "Lee Enterprises will manage Berkshire Hathaway newspaper and digital operations in 30 markets," Lee Enterprises, June 26, 2018 http://lee.net/financial/lee-enterprises-will-manage-berkshire-hathaway-newspaper-and-digital-operations/article_ebb48fee-78d3-11e8-a3a5-1fc0f14b0847.html

138   Lee Enterprises, 2017 Annual Report, January 24, 2018, https://www.sec.gov/Archives/edgar/data/58361/000005836117000053/a10k20179-24x1709242017act.htm

139   "Highlights from Berkshire Hathaway Q&A: On sticking by Wells Fargo, investing in guns, the future of newspapers, China and lots more," Omaha World-Herald, May 7, 2018, https://www.omaha.com/money/buffett/highlights-from-berkshire-hathaway-q-a-on-sticking-by-wells/article_ddda7042-726c-5f2f-a42e-0a7511eaa475.html

140   Steve Jordon, Brad Davis, "Warren Buffett hands reins of World-Herald, other Berkshire Hathaway newspapers to Iowa firm Lee Enterprises," Omaha World-Herald, June 28, 2018, https://www.omaha.com/money/warren-buffett-hands-reins-of-world-herald-other-berkshire-hathaway/article_b6712c29-6d8d-5ae6-b250-d524d9e1cccd.html

141   "Times-News, South Idaho Press, weeklies consolidate," Times-News, August 1, 2008, https://magicvalley.com/news/local/times-news-south-idaho-press-weeklies-consolidate/article_26ca293f-d840-562a-b3d9-cdc7e5b6620a.html

142   "Lee Enterprises to buy Dispatch-Argus of Moline/Rock Island," Dirks, Van Essen, Murray and April, June 19, 2017 http://dirksvanessen.com/press_releases/view/236/lee-enterprises-to-buy-dispatc/

143   Management Agreement, Lee Enterprises, Berkshire Hathaway, June 26, 2018, https://www.sec.gov/Archives/edgar/data/58361/000114036118029871/managementag.htm

144   Lee Enterprises, 2014 Annual Report, December 12, 2014, https://www.sec.gov/Archives/edgar/data/58361/000005836114000040/a10k20149-28x14.htm

145   Lee Enterprises, 2017 Annual Report, January 24, 2018,

146   Steve Jordon, Brad Davis, "Warren Buffett hands reins of World-Herald, other Berkshire Hathaway newspapers to Iowa firm   Lee Enterprises," Omaha World-Herald, June 28, 2018

147   Matt Wirz, "Warren Buffett Building Newspaper Empire?" Wall Street Journal, April 12, 2015, https://blogs.wsj.com/deals/2012/04/12/warren-buffett-building-newspaper-empire/

148   Lee Enterprises, 2013 Annual Report, December 13, 2013, https://www.sec.gov/Archives/edgar/data/58361/000005836113000038/a10k20139-29x13.htm
       See also: Tim Logan, "Buffett's Berkshire Hathaway raises stake in Lee newspapers," St. Louis Post-Dispatch, April 30, 2013, https://www.stltoday.com/business/local/buffett-s-berkshire-hatha-way-raises-stake-in-lee-newspapers/article_9d855231-f61f-5f67-892e-731d965d6e62.html

149   "Lee Enterprises pays off New Pulitzer Notes nearly two years early," June 25, 2015, http://lee.net/financial/lee-enterprises-pays-off-new-pulitzer-notes-nearly-two-years/article_318164a0-1b64-11e5-8571-9ba088a0a26d.html

150   Lee Enterprises, 2017 Annual Report, January 24, 2018,

151   Lee Enterprises, 2012 Annual Report, September 30, 2012

152   "Highlights from Berkshire Hathaway Q&A: On sticking by Wells Fargo, investing in guns, the future of newspapers, China and lots more," Omaha World-Herald, May 7, 2018, https://www.omaha.com/money/buffett/highlights-from-berkshire-hathaway-q-a-on-sticking-by-wells/article_ddda7042-726c-5f2f-a42e-0a7511eaa475.html

153   "Lee Enterprises will manage Berkshire Hathaway newspaper and digital operations in 30 markets," Lee Enterprises, June 26, 2018 http://lee.net/financial/lee-enterprises-will-manage-berkshire-hathaway-newspaper-and-digital-operations/article_ebb48fee-78d3-11e8-a3a5-1fc0f14b0847.html

154   "Our View: We'll be here to serve you for years to come," Times Leader Media Group, November 18, 2017, https://www.timesleader.com/opinion/682743/our-view-well-be-here-to-serve-you-for-years-to-come

155   "Versa Capital Announces the Formation of Civitas Media, LLC; Combines Four Community News Groups for Growth, Best Practices," Business Wire, September 11, 2012, https://www.businesswire.com/news/home/20120911006840/en/Versa-Capital-Announces-Formation-Civitas-Media-LLC

156   Aleksandrs Rozens, "DIPs Get Tough; Retail 'Always' Source of Distress, Says Versa's Segall," Bloomberg Brief, May 20, 2016, http://www.versa.com/docs/Bloomberg-article-5-20-16_REV.pdf

157   "Civitas Media CEO Announces He is Stepping Down," Business Wire, October 9, 2014, https://www.businesswire.com/news/home/20141009006229/en/Civitas-Media-CEO-Announces-Stepping

158   Troy Daily News Employee Review, Indeed, June 15, 2014, https://www.indeed.com/cmp/Troy-Daily-News/reviews?fcountry=ALL

159   "Civitas Media to close 8 weekly papers in NC, Ohio," Associated Press, July 18, 2013, http://www. thetimesnews.com/article/20130718/News/307189838

160   Thomas Gnau, "Company to close three Dayton-area papers," Dayton Daily News, July 18, 2013, https://www.daytondailynews.com/business/company-close-three-dayton-area-papers/IIGcTduOtl 98nNBctkDZTI/

161   Denise Allabaugh, "Times Leader parent company closes S.C. newspaper," Citizens' Voice, January 7, 2016, https://www.citizensvoice.com/news/times-leader-parent-company-closes-s-c-newspaper -1.1991958

162   United States Census Bureau: Cheraw, South Carolina https://www.census.gov/quickfacts/fact/table/ cherawtownsouthcarolina/PST045217

163   "Champion Media Acquires North Carolina and South Carolina Assets of Civitas Media," Dirks, Van Essen, Murray & April, June 15, 2017, http://dirksvanessen.com/press_releases/view/235/champion -media-acquires-north-/

164   "Adams Publishing Group Acquires Mount Airy Group from Champion Media," Cribb, Greene and Cope, October 26, 2017, https://www.editorandpublisher.com/news/adams-publishing-group -acquires-mount-airy-group-from-champion-media/

165   John Peters, "A change for the better," The Mount Airy News, July 2, 2017, https://www.mtairynews. com/opinion/52312/a-change-for-the-better

166   "Our View: We'll be here to serve you for years to come," Times Leader Media Group, November 18, 2017, https://www.timesleader.com/opinion/682743/our-view-well-be-here-to-serve-you-for-years- to-come

167   Denise Allabaugh, "Sale of Times Leader building pending," Citizens' Voice, October 3, 2017, https://www.citizensvoice.com/news/sale-of-times-leader-building-pending-1.2250578

168   John Peters, "A change for the better," The Mount Airy News, July 2, 2017, https://www.mtairynews. com/opinion/52312/a-change-for-the-better

169   Mark Evans, "I chose unemployment rather than work for 10/13 Communications," Tucson Sentinel, May 1, 2014, http://www.tucsonsentinel.com/opinion/report/050114_evans_itb/evans-i-chose-un employment-rather-than-work-10-13-communications/

170   "What Investment Companies Say About Themselves," Center for Innovation and Sustainability in Local Media, University of North Carolina at Chapel Hill, 2016, http://newspaperownership.com/ additional-material/investment-newspaper-owners-statements/

171   Dylan Smith, "Grimes leaving editor's desk at Explorer, ITB, Weekly," Tucson Sentinel, March 25, 2015, http://www.tucsonsentinel.com/local/report/032515_grimes/grimes-leaving-editors-desk -explorer-itb-weekly/

172   Mark Evans, "I chose unemployment rather than work for 10/13 Communications," Tucson Sentinel, May 1, 2014, http://www.tucsonsentinel.com/opinion/report/050114_evans_itb/evans-i-chose-un employment-rather-than-work-10-13-communications/

173   "Hearst Purchases Locally-Focused Houston Community Newspapers & Media Group," Hearst, July 29, 2016, http://www.hearst.com/newsroom/hearst-purchases-locally-focused-houston- community-newspapers-media-group

174   "Investing in Newspapers in 2018," Key Executives Mega-Conference Panel Discussion, San Diego, February 27, 2018 http://snpa.static2.adqic.com/static/2018MegaProgram.pdf

175   "Scott Wright buys 1013 Star Communication's suburban Dallas newspapers," Inland Press Association, November 17, 2016, http://www.inlandpress.org/stories/scott-wright -buys-1013-star-communications-suburban-dallas-newspapers,8130

176   "Times Media Group buys 2 Valley Newspapers," AZBIGMEDIA, January 28, 2016, https://azbigmedia. com/times-media-group-buys-2-valley-newspapers/

177   "Independent Newsmedia acquires 4 West Valley newspapers," June 21, 2016, https://www.scottsdaleindependent.com/news/independent-newsmedia-acquires-4-west-valley -newspapers/

178   UNC 2018 Database, Center for Innovation and Sustainability in Local Media

179   "About," Tucson Local Media, 2018, https://www.tucsonlocalmedia.com/site/about/

METHODOLOGY

The findings in this report are based on information in a comprehensive proprietary database of more than 9,000 local newspapers, created and maintained by the Center for Innovation and Sustainability in Local Media at the University of North Carolina at Chapel Hill. The data, collected over the past four years by faculty and researchers in the School of Media and Journalism, are derived from a variety of industry and government sources, supplemented with extensive reporting, fact-checking and multiple layers of verification. UNC maintains five separate databases on newspapers that were published in 2004, 2014, 2016, 2017 and 2018.

For this 2018 report, information on individual publications in the database has been cross-referenced with at least four sources. It includes statistics gleaned from two industry databases: Editor & Publisher DataBook (published 2004-2017) and E&P data accessed online for the years 2016-2018, as well as proprietary information collected and provided by the consulting firm BIA/Kelsey for the years 2004 and 2014. Researchers then verified these data with information obtained from 55 state, regional and national press associations and our own extensive independent online research, as well as interviews with staff at individual papers, when available. We have supplemented newspaper data with information from other industry sources, such as the Local Independent Online News (LION) association, the Alliance for Community Media (ACM), and the Pew Research Center. Layers of demographic, political and economic data from government sources were also added to the database. By visiting this website – **usnewsdeserts.com** – and using the interactive maps, researchers, as well as interested citizens, can drill down to the county level in all 50 states and compare how communities across the country have been affected by the closing of local newspapers.

Our database tracks the fate of the country's newspapers in recent years because newspapers have historically been the prime source of news and information that guides local decision-making of residents and government officials in most communities. Our research is concerned with identifying local newspapers that provide public-service journalism. Do they, for example, cover local government meetings? For our 2018 report, we intentionally excluded from our proprietary database shoppers, newsletters, specialty publications, advertising inserts and some zoned editions with very little locally produced public service journalism - even if they were identified as newspapers in other databases. This report does not attempt to assess the quality and quantity of news generated by all existing local news outlets, including not only newspapers, but also television and radio stations, as well as any online sites. This would require in-depth analysis of the content produced and distributed by these outlets. We recommend this as an additional research step to anyone seeking to determine the health of the local news ecosystem in a specific community.

Since this is one of the most comprehensive and up-to-date databases on newspapers, we make every effort to share it with serious academic and industry researchers who are pursuing related or relevant topics. If you would like access to our newspaper database, please contact us through the website.

Building and Refining the Database

As a result of the extra layers of verification that we have added since publishing our 2016 report (The Rise of the New Media Baron and the Emerging Threat of News Deserts), we have identified 300 local newspapers that existed in 2004 but were not listed in industry databases. Therefore, in our 2018 report, we have adjusted upward the number of newspapers in our 2004 database – to 8,891 newspapers (1,472 daily; 7,419 weekly).

Simultaneously, we have identified almost 600 papers that were stand-alone traditional newspapers in 2004, but by 2018 had evolved into shoppers, advertising supplements or specialty publications such as lifestyle magazines or business journals. Many of these are still listed in 2017 industry databases, but we removed them from UNC's 2018 database, since our focus is on identifying local newspapers. The 2018 report identifies 7,112 local newspapers in the country – 1,283 dailies and 5,829 weeklies – that are still being published. Each newspaper in the database has the following variables: year, name, frequency (daily/weekly), number of days published per week, city, state, parent media company and total circulation.

As was the case with the 2016 report, because our focus is on local newspapers, UNC also excluded from the 2018 report data on the country's largest national papers – The New York Times, The Wall Street Journal and USA Today – as well as shoppers, advertising supplements, magazines and other specialty publications. In total, 1,779 papers that were closed, merged or morphed into shoppers or specialty publications over the past 14 years were removed from the UNC database to arrive at the 2018 number.

The 2018 tally of 7,112 papers may overstate the number of stand-alone newspapers. Based on UNC's analysis of papers owned by the largest 25 chains, an estimated 10 to 15 percent of newspapers still listed in industry databases may be, in fact, zoned editions of larger papers. Nevertheless, these zoned editions were not removed from the 2018 tally, since they are still providing news coverage of important events and issues in their communities.

Despite adding multiple layers of verification, we realize the UNC Database is still prone to errors inherent in any large database, particularly one that depends in part on surveys and the accurate feedback of respondents. When we spotted errors, we corrected them in the database and will continue to update our analysis as new information becomes available. If you detect an error, please fill in and submit the "corrections" form available on our website, **usnewsdeserts.com**. In general, we update our most current year's database every quarter.

The Concept of News Deserts and Ghost Newspapers

In our 2018 report, we are introducing the concept of "ghost newspapers" and expanding our definition of "news deserts." Previously, we defined a news desert as a community without a newspaper. As a result of the dramatic shrinkage in the number of local news outlets in recent years, we have expanded our definition of news deserts to include communities where residents are facing significantly diminished access to the sort of important local news and information that feeds grassroots democracy.

As we compared our updated 2004 and 2018 databases and correlated them with numerous news stories and press releases, we noted that a number of traditional stand-alone newspapers had become shells, or "ghosts," of their former selves. They are no longer providing residents in communities large and small with the news they needed to make informed decisions about a range of important issues that could affect their quality of life.

We identified two types of ghost newspapers: the once-iconic weeklies that merged with larger dailies and evolved into shoppers or specialty publications, and the metro and regional state papers that have dramatically scaled back their newsroom staffing, as well as their government coverage of inner-city and suburban communities, as well as rural areas. As noted above in "Building and Refining the Database," UNC removed from the 2018 database 600 weeklies that had become shoppers or specialty publications since 2004. However, we did not remove the larger metro and regional state papers, but estimated the number — at least 1,000 – by comparing industry statistics on newsroom staffing and circulation to news articles about the size of an individual paper's newsroom staffing in 2004 compared with 2018. To determine definitively whether a large daily is fulfilling its civic journalism role of informing a community on important issues, much more research – including in-depth analysis of published content – is needed. Having raised the issue, we leave that to other researchers to determine if an individual paper is a "ghost."

Dealing with Circulation Limitations

There is currently no widely accepted and easily accessible tracking system of online readership data, especially for the thousands of local papers in small and mid-sized markets. Therefore, print circulation is used as a proxy for measuring the decline in both the reach and influence of traditional newspapers.

The print circulation figures in our database come with limitations. Some circulation figures are audited and verified; others are self-reported. Therefore, in our 2018 database, we've added additional verification steps and information in an attempt to be as transparent as possible about where we are getting the numbers. We also noted whether the reported circulation is free or paid circulation.

When possible, we use circulation numbers from the Alliance for Audited Media (AAM). AAM is the industry leader in media verification and specializes in verifying circulation metrics for publishers. However, only 13 percent of papers in the UNC Database subscribe to AAM audits. Additionally, the reported AAM numbers for the large dailies often lag behind the audit by a couple of years.

Because news organizations must pay AAM to verify their circulation statistics, many small papers do not use the service and instead self-report. If there are no AAM data, UNC relied on self-reported newspaper circulation from a variety of sources (E&P, state press associations and independent research). Self-reported circulation data are problematic, since UNC researchers observed that a significant number of newspapers report the same circulation across multiple years. However, self-reported numbers are the only option available for many small weekly papers.

U.S. and State Maps

For the 2018 report, UNC created interactive maps for the country and all 50 states, plus the District of Columbia. The maps in this report, and in its online version, provide insights into the risk of news deserts in thousands of communities across the country. By visiting **usnewsdeserts.com**, researchers can analyze data (demographics, political leanings, number of news outlets) down to the county level for all 50 states. UNC researchers used government data to pinpoint the locations of newspapers as accurately as possible. Often, both the BIA/Kelsey and E&P 2014 databases incorrectly listed the parent company or city location for many newspapers, especially the smaller ones. UNC researchers attempted to review and correct errors. The UNC Database uses the newspaper's office as the physical address for mapping purposes.

To identify whether newspapers were located in a rural or an urban area, each was assigned to a corresponding group from the U.S. Department of Agriculture's Rural-Urban Continuum Codes (RUCC) based on the county in which they were located. According to RUCC codes, communities in groups one though three were classified as metro areas. All others were classified as rural. Additionally, U.S. Census information on demographics (income, age, population makeup, etc.) was merged into the database, as well as information from state election boards and industry sources such as the Local Independent Online News (LION) association. We also overlaid the USDA's information to locate counties in food deserts. The USDA defines a food desert as "parts of the country vapid of fresh fruit, vegetables, and other healthful whole foods, usually found in impoverished areas due to a lack of grocery stores, farmers' markets and healthy food providers."

For national and state maps, visit **usnewsdeserts.com**.

Tracking Sales, Mergers and Closures

UNC tracks changes in a newspaper's ownership, as well as closures and mergers, through news accounts and press releases. We define a closure as a newspaper that is no longer published and a merger as a newspaper that has been combined with another publication. Often the two merged papers initially have a combined name, but eventually the name of the smaller paper is eliminated. We tracked mergers and acquisitions in the newspaper industry from 2004 to 2018 and assessed corporate strategies by identifying and examining:

- Publicly available corporate documents, including quarterly and annual reports released by the individual companies and press releases by Dirks, Van Essen, Murray & April and Cribb, Greene & Cope, two of the leading merger and acquisition firms in the U.S. newspaper industry.
- Numerous news articles about individual purchases and business decisions.
- Statements made by executives that were in press releases, news articles or industry presentations.
- Reports and interviews with industry representatives and analysts.

There are limitations to all of the above sources. Press releases, news articles, statements made by news executives and reports from industry analysts often list by title only the sales of the largest and most prominent newspapers, usually dailies. The weeklies involved in the sale, as well as specialty publications (including shoppers and business journals) are often grouped together and reported as a single number. That is why we try to check all announcements of sales against publicly available documents and corporate websites.

We track updates to the industry through the Twitter account **@businessofnews** and post important developments on our website, **usnewsdeserts.com**. For the past three years, we've updated the current year's database on a quarterly basis. The final update of the 2018 database will occur in January 2019, when all transactions that occurred in the fourth quarter of the previous year will be recorded.

Media Groupings

Similar to our 2016 report, UNC categorized the largest 25 newspaper owners into one of three categories: private companies, publicly traded companies and investment companies.

- **Private Companies:** This group includes large companies, such as Hearst Corp., which own a portfolio of media that include an array of media formats. They not only own print publications, but cable networks and digital enterprises as well. This category can also include smaller companies like Boone Newspapers, which owns fewer than 100 publications in small and mid-sized communities throughout the South.
- **Public Companies:** This group includes publicly traded companies such as Gannett, Lee Enterprises and McClatchy.
- **Investment Companies:** This category has arisen in the past decade and has a different ownership philosophy and financial structure from the traditional newspaper owners. Owners in this group can be either private or public, but the key distinctions in investment company ownership are the companies' business philosophies and financial structures, which differ significantly from those of traditional newspaper chains. Companies were classified in this category if they met at least five of the eight characteristics in the chart below:

HOW INVESTMENT COMPANIES DIFFER FROM TRADITIONAL NEWSPAPER CHAINS

CHARACTERISTICS	NewMedia/ GateHouse	Digital First	CNHI	Civitas	tronc/ Tribune	BH Media	10/13 Communications
The stated emphasis of the parent company is to maximize shareholder return on investment	X	X	X	X	X	X	X
Many properties were acquired as a group from other media companies through either purchase of entire companies or divisions.	X	X	X	X	X	X	X
Majority financial and/or operational control of the firm is held by a small number of institutional shareholders, such as lenders, private equity firms or investment fund managers.	X	X	X	X	X	X	X
The company was formed or incorporated within the past two decades and is a relative newcomer to newspaper ownership.	X	X	X	X		X	X
The newspaper holdings are part of a portfolio of non-newspaper companies.	X	X	X	X		X	X
There has been much movement of individual newspapers within portfolios.	X	X	X	X	X		
There have been two or more financial restructurings, including bankruptcy reorganization, a rebranding after selling the company or flips between public and private ownership.	X	X		X	X		
A private equity company, a hedge fund or penion fund has at some point during the past decade owned all or a significant portion of the enterprise.	X	X	X	X	X		X

SOURCE: UNC DATABASE

About the Editor & Publisher and BIA/Kelsey Databases

Editor & Publisher began publishing an annual Newspaper DataBook in 1921. The DataBook has information on more than 25,000 companies and more than 160 data fields. Data are collected through mail and email surveys, supplemented with telephone research. BIA/Kelsey, a research and advisory company, focused on local advertising and marketing, began tracking newspaper ownership in 2004. The organization employs a telemarketing team that calls individual newspapers and collects information from employee respondents.

CONTRIBUTORS

The Expanding News Desert and the website, **usnewsdeserts.com**, was produced by Center for Innovation and Sustainability in Local Media in the School of Media and Journalism at the University of North Carolina at Chapel Hill.

About the Author

Penelope Muse Abernathy, formerly an executive with The Wall Street Journal and The New York Times, is the Knight Chair in Journalism and Digital Media Economics. She is the author of Saving Community Journalism: The Path to Profitability (UNC Press: 2014) and co-author of The Strategic Digital Media Entrepreneur (Wiley Blackwell: 2018).

About the Center

UNC's Center for Innovation and Sustainability in Local Media supports existing and start-up news organizations through its dissemination of applied research and the development of digital tools and solutions. The Center supports the economic and business research of UNC's Knight Chair in Journalism and Digital Media Economics. It also supports faculty and students associated with the Reese News Lab, which designs, tests and adapts digital tools for use in small and mid-sized newsrooms. The Center is funded by grants from the Knight Foundation and UNC.

Researchers

Erinn Whitaker, Senior Researcher and Writer
Alex Dixon, Research Assistant
Jill Fontaine, Research Specialist
Nicole McNeill, Research Specialist

Student Researchers include:
    Kriste Patrow '19 (Ph.D.), Chris Gentilviso '19 (M.A.), Natasha Townsend '19, Harris Wheless '19,
    Ian McDaniel '19, Paige Moose '20, Kristen Marino '18, Vaughn Stewart '17 (Ph.D.),
    Tatiana Quirogo '17 (M.A.), Lindsey Carbonell '17

Other Significant Contributors

Craig Anderson, Project Director, Center for Innovation and Sustainability in Local Media
Leonardo Castanedo, Data Visualization Specialist
Bill Cloud, Associate Professor of Journalism (Ret.)
Michele Kisthardt, Hudson Integrated Marketing, Communications Advisor
Michael McElroy, Adjunct Professor
Carol Zarker, Communications Project Manager, Center for Innovation and Sustainability in Local Media

UNC School of Media and Journalism

Susan R. King, Dean
Louise Spieler, Senior Associate Dean

CPSIA information can be obtained
at www.ICGtesting.com
Printed in the USA
LVHW071619110919

630734LV00017B/418/P